Chic&Easy
Beading
Vol. 2

KALMBACH
BOOKS

Printed in the United States of America

07 08 09 10 11 12 13 14 15   10 9 8 7 6 5 4

Publisher's Cataloging-In-Publication Data
(Prepared by The Donohue Group, Inc.)

Chic & easy beading.

   v. [1-2] : ill. ; cm.
   ISBN: 0-87116-225-3

1. Beadwork. 2. Jewelry making. I. Title: Chic and easy beading

TT860 .C48 2006
745.594/2

ISBN 978-0-87116-225-0

Senior Art Director: Lisa Bergman
Book design: Sabine Beaupré
Editors: Julia Gerlach, Cheryl Phelan, Lesley Weiss

Acknowledgments: Linda Augsburg, Tea Benduhn, Paulette Biedenbender, Mindy Brooks, Karin Buckingham, Terri Field, Jim Forbes, Naomi Fujimoto, Lora Groszkiewicz, Judith Hill, Kellie Jaeger, Diane Jolie, Kelly Katlaps, Patti Keipe, Alice Korach, Pat Lantier, Tonya Limberg, Debbie Nishihara, Carrie Rohloff, Carole Ross, Candice St. Jacques, Maureen Schimmel, Kristin Schneidler, Lisa Schroeder, Terri Torbeck, Elizabeth Weber, Bill Zuback

Contents

Jewelry Sets

Other Accessories

Introduction

Beading is growing increasingly popular and it's no wonder — even a handful of beads unleashes infinite possibilities. Beaders can play with colors, materials, and techniques to express themselves creatively. It's a hobby that can fit any pocketbook, and allows anyone to be an artist.

Beginning beaders are often surprised by how easy and fun it is to make beautiful accessories that match an outfit or a mood. Even if you've never strung a bracelet, you can complete your first project quickly and discover how rewarding it is to make your own jewelry. In fact, you may find it difficult to stop!

The first volume of *Chic&Easy* was compiled from the first two *Chic&Easy* annual special editions of *Bead&Button* magazine. The overwhelming popularity of that book, with its emphasis on style and ease of construction, helped to launch a new beading magazine, *BeadStyle*, which emphasizes jewelry that is fast, fashionable, and fun.

Chic&Easy, Vol. 2, has been compiled from the third and final *Chic&Easy* special edition, and also includes a selection of projects from *BeadStyle* and *Bead&Button* magazines. All the projects are simple and stylish, and include step-by-step photos to guide you through the process. Our illustrated Basics section and editor-tested instructions will have you creating your own beautiful beaded jewelry in no time. With a wide variety of projects — necklaces, bracelets, earrings, rings, brooches and more — this collection has something to fit everyone's taste and budget.

Turn the page to review materials and techniques, then pick your favorite projects and get started.

Essential materials for getting started

Key supplies

What does it take to make beautiful jewelry? The secret is knowing which tools and materials will give you the best results.

Tools

There are excellent tools for making jewelry available in bead shops, catalogs, and on the Internet. Hardware stores and craft stores also yield great finds.

A. Roundnose pliers have smooth, tapered, conical jaws and are used to form loops in wire. Choose a pair with narrow jaws so you can turn small loops when needed.

B. Chainnose pliers have smooth, flat inner jaws, and the tips taper to a point so you can get into small spaces. Use them for gripping wire, closing bead tips, and for opening and closing loops and rings. (Hardware-store pliers often have ridges on their jaws. Chainnose pliers for jewelry and wirework must have flat inner surfaces.)

C. On diagonal wire cutters, the backs of the blades meet squarely, yielding a flat-cut surface. The fronts make a pointed cut. Always cut with the back against the section you want to finish so that the wire end will be flat. Never use jewelry wire cutters on memory wire, which is extremely hard; use heavy-duty cutters or bend the memory wire until it breaks.

D. Crimping pliers have two grooves in their jaws — one presses an indentation into the crimp bead, the other folds the crimp into a compact, cylindrical shape.

E. Use thread snips or small scissors for cutting bead-stringing cord.

F. An awl has a handle and a sharp, pointed metal tip. It is the easiest tool to use when knotting between beads.

G. A twisted wire needle is simply a length of fine wire folded in half and twisted tightly together. It has a large, open eye at the fold, which is easy to thread, and it accommodates thicker cords than conventional beading needles.

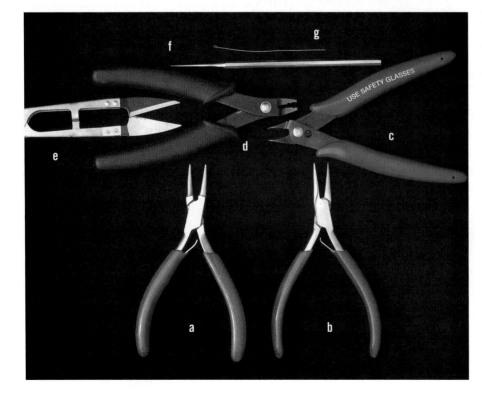

Findings

Findings are the components that link beads into a piece of jewelry. Always buy the best you can afford. Some inexpensive base metal findings may soon discolor. Sterling silver and gold-filled findings are slightly more expensive, but they look good for many years.

A. A head pin looks like a thick, blunt sewing pin with a flat or decorative head on one end to keep the beads from falling off. Head pins come in different gauges and in lengths ranging from 1-3 in. (2.5-8cm).

B. Eye pins are like head pins with a round loop on one end instead of a head. Once you are comfortable making wire loops, you can easily make your own eye pins.

C. A jump ring is a small wire circle or oval with a split that you can twist open and closed. It connects loops with loops or loops with other findings. A soldered jump ring has had its opening soldered shut and is often used as part of a clasp.

D. Split rings look like tiny key rings. They are more secure than jump rings and a good substitute for them.

E. Crimp beads are round or tube-shaped beads designed for use with flexible beading wire. They can be flattened with chainnose pliers or folded into a roll with crimping pliers.

F. Bead tips or calottes are small metal beads primarily used to link a strand of beads on cord to a clasp. Bead tips come in a clamshell shape or as a basket. Clamshell bead tips close over the knot and hide it. The knot rests against the basket in basket-shaped bead tips.

G. Clasps come in an extensive range of shapes, sizes, materials, and prices. Some of the most common are toggles, consisting of a ring and a bar; lobster claws and spring rings, which open when you push on a tiny lever; S-hooks; and hook-and-eye clasps.

H. Earrings also come in many shapes, sizes, and styles, including posts, French hooks, kidney wires, and hoops. Post earrings require a loop if you plan to attach any kind of dangle.

I. Cones have openings at both ends, one large and one small. They are ideal for concealing the knotted ends of a tassel or multistrand necklace.

Stringing materials

There is a steady supply of new stringing materials available to beaders, so experiment to find the cords you prefer. Look for products that are durable, come in several weights or sizes, and offer a good selection of colors.

Flexible beading wire consists of very fine wires twisted or braided together and covered with a smooth plastic coating. The wires come in several diameters, depending on brand, but range from .010 in. (.3mm) to .036 in. (.9mm). Most come in 7-wire, 19- or 21-wire, and 49-wire grades. The 49-wire beading wire is the highest grade and the most expensive. Finish beading wire projects with crimp beads.

Beading cords and threads come in many materials, but nylon is the most common since it is both strong and supple. Cord size is indicated either by a number or letter — the lower the number or letter, the thinner the cord. (The exception is O, which is very thin.) Use these doubled for extra security.

High-tech fishing lines, particularly Fireline, are a popular choice for stringing. They're strong, fray-resistant, and won't stretch. Never string beads on monofilament because it becomes brittle over time.

Traditionally, pearls are strung on silk, but many of the new nylons are almost as supple and much less fragile.

Wire is used to make clasps, dangles, and many decorative elements. It is sold by gauge, with thinner-gauge wires having higher numbers. For making jewelry, common sizes are 16- to 28-gauge. Sterling silver and gold-filled wire are designated dead soft or half hard. The two are often interchangeable, but half-hard wire holds its shape better in the thinner gauges.

Memory wire is steel spring wire. It comes in several sizes and can be used without clasps to make coiled bracelets, necklaces, and rings.

Basics

Knots

Half-hitch knot

Come out of a bead and form a loop perpendicular to the thread between beads. Bring the needle under the thread away from the loop. Then go back over the thread and through the loop. Pull gently so the knot doesn't tighten prematurely.

Overhand knot

Make a loop in the cord and bring the end that crosses on top behind the loop. Then pull it through to the front.

Square knot

1. Cross the left-hand cord over the right-hand cord, and then bring it under the right-hand cord from back to front. Pull it up in front so both ends are facing upward.

2. Cross right over left, forming a loop, and go through the loop, again from back to front. Pull the ends to tighten the knot.

Surgeon's knot

Cross the right end over the left end, then bring it under the left cord. Go over and under again. Cross the left end over the right end and go through once. Pull the ends to tighten.

Wire & metal techniques

Crimping

Thread a crimp bead and a large-hole bead on one end of a length of flexible beading wire. Go through one end of the clasp. Bring the wire back through both beads. Slide the bead and crimp close to the clasp, leaving a small space. Then crimp the crimp bead using one of the following methods:

Flattened crimp

1. Hold the crimp using the tip of your chainnose pliers. Squeeze the pliers firmly to flatten the crimp.

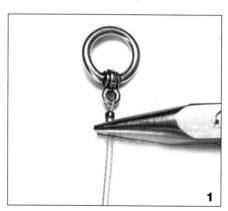

2. Tug the clasp to make sure the crimp has a solid grip on the wire. If the wire slides, repeat the steps with a new crimp.

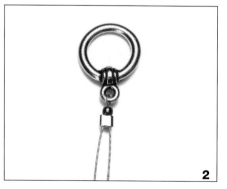

Folded crimp

1. Position the crimp bead in the notch closest to the crimping pliers' handle.

2. Separate the wires and firmly squeeze the crimp.

3. Move the crimp into the notch at the pliers' tip and hold the crimp as shown. Squeeze the crimp bead, folding it in half at the indentation.

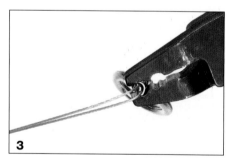

4. Test that the folded crimp is secure.

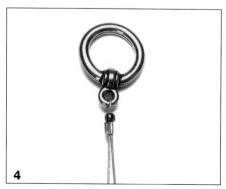

Loops: opening and closing

1. Hold the jump ring with two pairs of chainnose pliers or chainnose and roundnose pliers, as shown.

2. To open the jump ring, bring the tips of one pair of pliers toward you and push the tips of the other pair away.

3. String materials on the open jump ring. Reverse the steps to close it.

Plain loops

1. Trim the wire ⅜ in. (1cm) above the top bead. Make a right angle bend close to the bead.

2. Grab the wire's tip with roundnose pliers. Roll the wire to form a half circle. Release the wire.

3. Reposition the pliers in the loop and continue rolling.

4. The finished loop should form a centered circle above the bead.

Wrapped loops

1. Make sure you have at least 1¼ in. (3.2cm) of wire above the bead. With the tip of your chainnose pliers, grasp the wire directly above the bead. Bend the wire (above the pliers) into a right angle.

2. Using roundnose pliers, position the jaws in the bend.

3. Bring the wire over the top jaw of the roundnose pliers.

4. Reposition the pliers' lower jaw snugly into the loop. Curve the wire downward around the bottom of the roundnose pliers. This is the first half of a wrapped loop.

5. Position the chainnose pliers' jaws across the loop.

6. Wrap the wire around the wire stem, covering the stem between the loop and the top bead. Trim the excess wire and press the cut end close to the wraps with chainnose pliers.

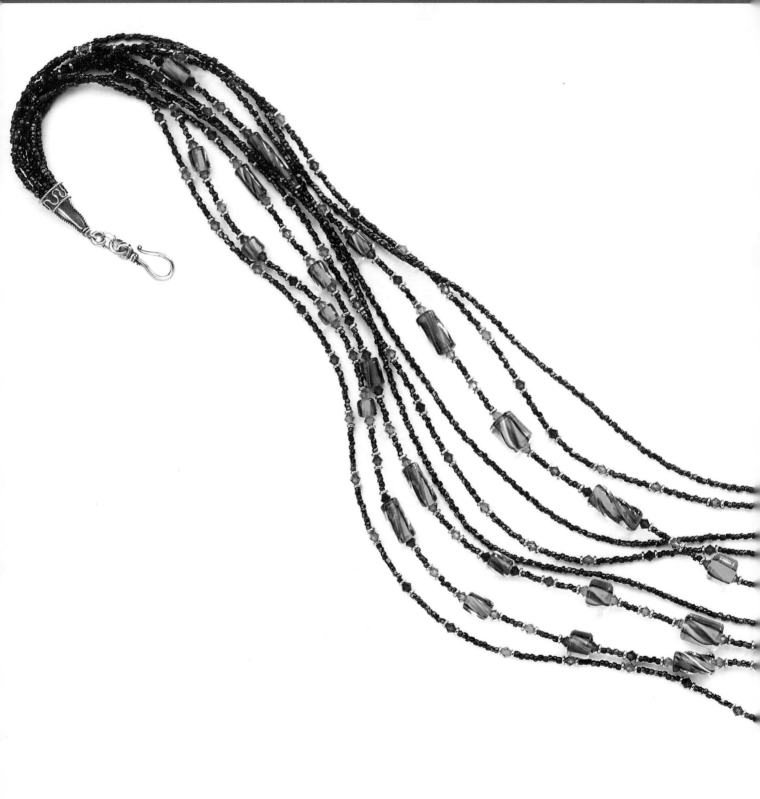

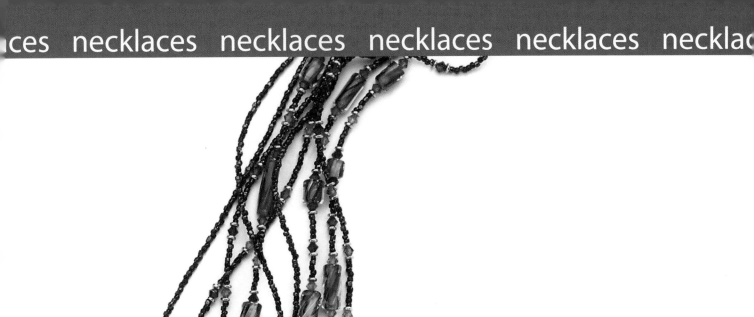

Necklaces
Chapter 1

A cut above

String a richly textured necklace of
faceted stones and sterling silver

1. Cut a 26-in. (66cm) length of flexible beading wire.

2. String the silver pendant to the center of the wire. If the pendant has a large bail, fill the bail with small beads (**photo a**).

3. String four rondelles and a silver spacer on both sides of the pendant. If the rondelles don't sit flush against the bail, string a silver spacer between the pendant and rondelles (**photo b**).

4. String four rondelles and a 10–18mm silver bead on both ends (**photo c**).

5. String a repeating pattern of four rondelles and a silver spacer on both ends until the necklace is about 1½-in. (3.8cm) shorter than the desired length.

6. Tape the ends and check the fit. Add or remove beads equally on both sides, if necessary, to keep the pendant centered.

7. String one or more silver spacers, a crimp bead, and a 2mm round silver bead. Go through the loop on one of the clasp components and back through the 2mm bead, the crimp bead, and silver spacers (**photo d**).

8. Tighten the wire and crimp the crimp bead (Basics, p. 8). Trim the excess wire.

9. Repeat steps 7–8 to attach the remaining clasp half to the other end of the necklace.

— *Rupa Balachandar*

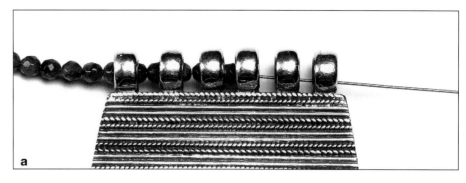

a

b

c

d

materials
necklace 19½ in. (50cm)

- sterling silver pendant (rupab.com)
- 16-in. (41cm) strand 12mm faceted stone rondelles
- **2** 10–18mm sterling silver beads
- **16–20** 4–8mm sterling silver spacer beads
- **2** 2mm round silver beads (optional)
- seed beads or small beads to fill bail on pendant (optional)
- clasp
- **2** crimp beads
- flexible beading wire, size .014
Tools: crimping pliers, diagonal wire cutters

Cabana necklace

Pair Caribbean-blue turquoise with sterling silver shells for a casual, summer necklace. Woven multistrands lighten the sides and add an unexpected twist. You can customize the project by playing with the length or eliminating elements to create the perfect cruisewear accompaniment.

Center

1. Cut 16 in. (40cm) of flexible beading wire.

2. Center 3 in. (7.6cm) of turquoise discs on the wire.

3. Tape one end of the wire to secure the beads. On the other end, string spacers, large shell beads, and turquoise as shown in **photo a**.

4. String a crimp bead and a jump ring. Go back through the crimp and spacer (**photo b**). Tighten the wire, then

crimp the crimp bead and trim the excess wire.

Multistrand section

1. Thread a needle with 2 yd. (1.8m) of Fireline. Center a jump ring on the Fireline and secure it in place with two square knots (Basics, p. 8). Dot the knots with glue, let dry, then trim the tail.

2. String 2½ in. (6.3cm) of silver and clear cylinder beads in random order

a

b

c

f

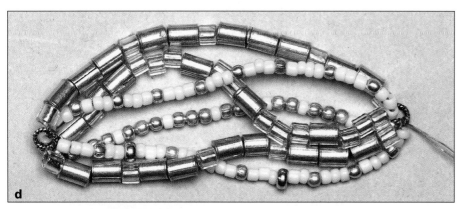

d

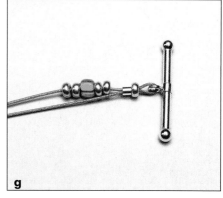

g

e

materials

20-in. (51cm) necklace

- 6 16mm sterling silver shells
- 32 14mm turquoise discs
- 8 11mm sterling silver shells
- 36 3mm flat spacers
- 150-180 2mm silver balls
- 50-60 5mm silver cylinder beads
- 1g Japanese cylinder beads, size 8º, clear
- 2 seed beads, size 5º, aqua
- 1g seed beads, size 14º, white
- 6 crimp beads
- toggle clasp
- flexible beading wire, .014–.019
- Fireline, 10 lb. test
- beading needles, #12
- G-S Hypo cement

Tools: chainnose or crimping pliers

and then a jump ring (**photo c**).

3. Secure the jump ring with two overhand knots (Basics).

4. Repeat step 2. Tie the Fireline to the first jump ring with two overhand knots, as before. Repeat step 2 again, this time tying the Fireline to the second jump ring.

5. String three more strands as before, using white 14º seed beads and silver balls (**photo d**).

6. String three silver balls, then go through one of the beads on any strand (**photo e**). Repeat until you reach the jump ring, then connect the strand with two overhand knots.

7. Repeat step 6 three times. Dot all the knots with glue, let dry, then trim

the tail. Connect one jump ring to the jump ring in the center portion.

Back

1. Cut 8 in. (20cm) of flexible beading wire.

2. String the other jump ring in the multistrand section, a crimp, and a spacer. Go back through the crimp and spacer. Tighten the wire, then crimp the crimp bead and trim the tail.

3. String spacers, small shells, and turquoise discs as shown in **photo f**.

4. After the last shell, string two spacers, an aqua 5º, two spacers, a crimp, a spacer, and the toggle's loop. Go back through the spacer, crimp (**photo g**), spacers, and 5º. Tighten the wire, then

crimp the crimp bead and trim the end.

6. Remove the tape and make the other side of the necklace to mirror the first.

— Diane Jolie

Great lengths

Color wheels of furnace glass sparkle
in draped strands

a

b

Furnace glass strands

Lay out three rows of furnace glass, as follows: Use 17 beads
in the longest row, 15 in the middle, and 13 in the shortest.
Refer to the photo on p. 16 for spacing and lay out the beads
in a pleasing arrangement.

Longest strand

1. Cut a strand of beading wire 45 in. (1.1m) long. Secure one
end temporarily with a clamp or tape.

2. String a spacer, a crystal, a spacer, ½ in. (1.3 cm) of seed
beads, a spacer, a crystal, a furnace glass bead, a crystal, a
spacer, and ½ in. of seed beads (**photo a**). Repeat this sequence
until you've used all 17 furnace glass beads, ending with a

c

d

e

spacer, a crystal, and a spacer. String up to 6 in. (15cm) of seed beads equally on each end, and secure the ends as before.

Middle strand
Cut a strand of beading wire 42 in. (1m) long. Repeat step 2 of the longest strand, using 15 furnace glass beads instead of 17.

Shortest strand
Cut a strand of beading wire 39 in. (99cm) long. Repeat step 2 of the longest strand, using 13 furnace glass beads instead of 17.

Crystal strands
Longest strand
1. Cut a strand of beading wire 44 in. (1.1m) long.
2. String a spacer, a crystal, a spacer, and ¾ in. (2cm) of seed beads (**photo b**).
3. Repeat until you have completed 34 crystal segments.
4. Add seed beads to each end as before.

Middle strand
Make the middle strand the same same way as the longest strand, with the following changes: The middle beading wire is 41 in. (1m) long and has 31 crystal segments.

Shortest strand
The shortest strand is 38 in. (97cm) long and has 29 crystal segments.

Seed bead strands
String three strands of seed beads in the following lengths: The longest, 43 in. (1.1m), the middle, 40 in. (1m), and the shortest, 37 in. (94cm).

Finish the strands
Add or remove seed beads equally on each end of the strands until you have a pleasing arrangement and the right fit. String a crimp bead on each end, go back through the crimp bead, and tighten the beading wire until only a small loop remains. Crimp the crimp bead (Basics, p. 8) and trim the tails.

Assembling the necklace
1. Start a wrapped loop (Basics) on 4 in. (10cm) of wire. Slide one end of all nine strands into the loop (**photo c**).
2. Finish the wrapped loop and slide the cone on the wire and over all the strands (**photo d**).
3. Start a wrapped loop above the cone and slide your clasp or jump ring into the loop before you finish the wraps (**photo e**).
4. Repeat steps 1–3 on the other end of the necklace.

— *Judy Walker*

materials
necklace 30 in. (76cm)
- **45** furnace glass beads in various sizes and colors (Glasscapes, mingoandasho.com)
- hank of plain or faceted seed beads, size 15º–8º
- **400** 3–4mm silver spacer beads
- **232** 4mm Swarovski bicone crystals
- **2** Bali silver cones
- clasp
- flexible beading wire, .014–.015
- **18** crimp beads
- 8 in. (20cm) 16-gauge silver wire
- **4** 4mm jump rings (optional)

Tools: chainnose and roundnose pliers, crimping pliers, wire cutters, beading board (optional)

Surprise inside

Combine simulated opal with blue jade and crystals for an elegant necklace

1. Determine the finished length of your necklace. This one is 19 in. (48cm). Add 6 in. (15cm) and cut a piece of beading wire to that length.

2. String a rondelle, two 15ºs, a 5mm crystal, two 15ºs, a rondelle, the opal drop bead, a rondelle, two 15ºs, a 5mm crystal, two 15ºs, and a rondelle. Slide them to the center (**photo a**).

3. Continue stringing the repeating pattern (two 15ºs, a crystal, two 15ºs, a rondelle) on both sides of the necklace until you reach the desired length.

4. On one end, string two 6º dichro-lined seed beads, a crimp bead, a size 11º seed bead, and one half of the clasp. Come back through the 11º, the crimp bead, and the 6ºs (**photo c**). Pull snug and crimp the crimp bead. (Basics, p. 8). Trim the excess wire.

5. Repeat step 5 to attach the other half of the toggle to the other end.

— *Debbie Nishihara*

materials

necklace 19 in. (48cm)

- opal drop borosilicate bead (KBGlassworks, 505-254-2257, kbglassworks.com)
- strand 10mm blue dyed jade faceted rondelles (Eclectica, 262-641-0910, eclecticabeads.com)
- **28** 5mm Swarovski crystal bicones, olivine AB
- seed beads
  4 size 6º, blue/green dichro-lined (Beyond Beadery, 800-840-5548, beyondbeadery.com)
  2 size 11º, green metallic
  3g size 15º, green metallic
- flexible beading wire, .014
- textured heart toggle clasp (Scottsdale Bead Supply, 480-945-5988, scottsdalebead.com)
- **2** crimp beads

Tools: crimping pliers, wire cutters

a

b

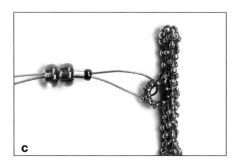

c

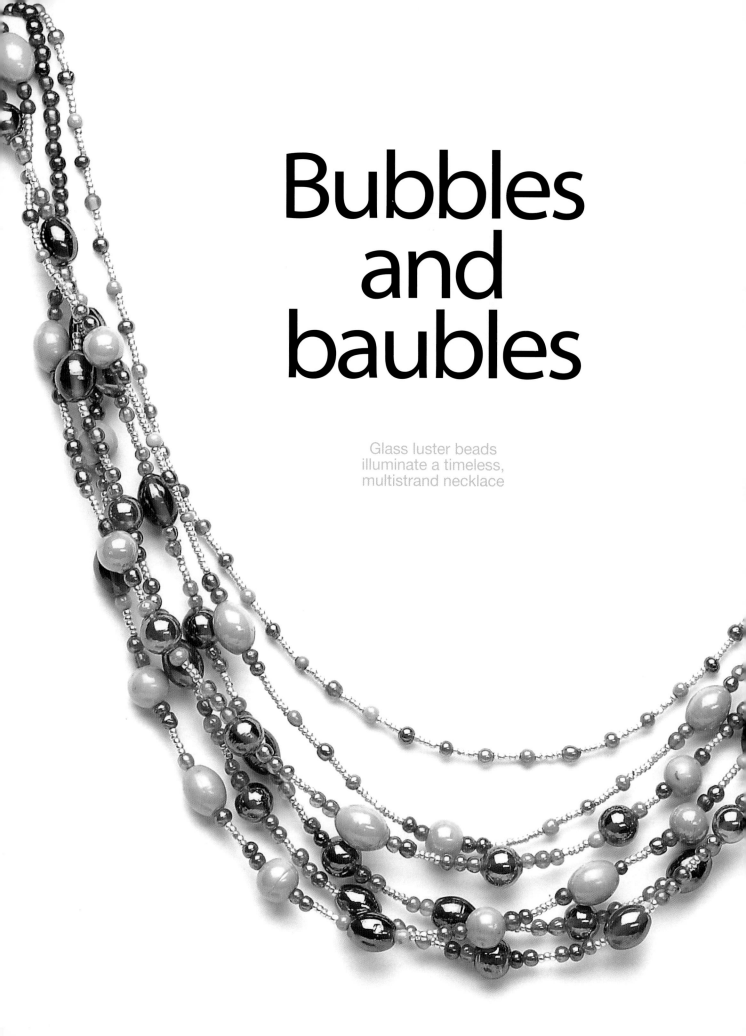

Bubbles and baubles

Glass luster beads
illuminate a timeless,
multistrand necklace

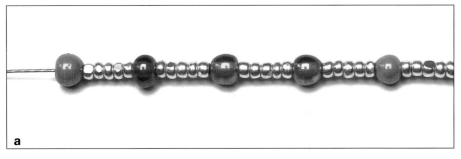

a

b

c

d

e

f

1. Determine the finished length of your necklace. (These necklace strands range in length from 16½–20 in./42–51cm). Add 6 in. (15cm) to the measurement of your shortest strand and cut one piece of beading wire to that length. Cut five additional wires, each 1 in. (2.5cm) longer than the previous one.

2. String a pattern of 4mm beads and seed beads on the shortest strand (**photo a**). Make this strand about 1 in. shorter than the finished length to allow for the clasp.

3. On the next longest wire, string a pattern of seed beads, 4mm beads, and a few 12mm beads (**photo b**). This strand should be about 1 in. longer than the previous one.

4. Hold the third and fourth longest wires together. String smaller beads over both strands for 4 in. (10cm). Separate the strands and continue this pattern for about 11 in. (23cm) on the shorter strand. Work a new pattern on the longer strand for about 12 in. (31cm), using more of the larger beads (**photo c**). Join the strands and repeat the first

pattern over both wires. The shorter of these two strands should be about 1 in. longer than the strand made in step 2.

5. Repeat step 4 with the last pair of wires, increasing the length as before (**photo d**).

6. Working one end at a time, string a spacer bead, a crimp bead, and a spacer on each wire or pair of wires. Take each wire through a soldered jump ring and back through the beads just strung (**photo e**). Tighten the wires. Repeat on the other end.

7. Check the fit and add or remove beads as necessary. Crimp the crimp beads (see Basics, p. 8) and trim the excess wire.

8. Attach the jump ring to the clasp with a split ring (**photo f**). Repeat on the other end.

— *Karin Buckingham*

materials
necklace 20 in. (51cm)
- **300 or more** 4mm round glass beads, 2 colors
- **26 or more** 8mm round glass beads, 2 colors
- **22 or more** 12mm oval glass beads, 2 colors
- **10g** seed beads, size 11º
- **16** 3mm spacer beads
- **2** 6mm soldered jump rings
- **2** 6mm split rings
- **8** crimp beads
- clasp
- flexible beading wire, .019

Tools: chainnose or crimping pliers, diagonal wire cutters, split ring pliers (optional)

EDITOR'S NOTE: This multistrand design easily accommodates style changes. Try using more or fewer strands, longer or shorter lengths, and beads in multiple finishes and colors.

Donut deluxe

Create a striking necklace using a strong combination of colorful gemstones

This necklace was inspired by the wonderful serpentine donut that looks like ancient carved jade. Two strands of luscious, yellow amber disk beads are combined with stones that bridge the gap between the amber and the donut in color and shape. The end result is this strong, somewhat ethnic, combination.

1. Cut the flexible beading wire into four 2-ft. (61cm) lengths. Clamp the end of one piece in a hemostat. Start stringing with 5 silver spacers, then alternately string a carnelian and a spacer, ending with 5 spacers. The strand should be about 17¾ in. (45cm) long.

2. On the second wire, randomly string about 2½ in. (6.3cm) of amber-colored seed beads between the amber beads. Start and end with a seed bead. Repeat for the second amber strand. Each strand is about 18½ in. (47cm) long.

3. On the fourth wire, randomly string green seed beads between the jade beads to make an 18½-in. long strand. Start and end with a seed bead.

4. String a crimp bead on the amber and jade strands. Leaving 2–3-in. (5–8cm) wire tails, crimp the crimp bead (Basics, p. 8). Braid the strands so the final length matches the carnelian strand. String a crimp bead over the wires and against the beads. Crimp the crimp bead. If necessary, remove a bead or add a few spacers to the ends of the carnelian strand.

5. Cut two 4-in. (10cm) lengths of sterling wire. Make a wrapped loop (Basics) at one end of each wire that fits inside the cones.

6. Crimp one end of the carnelian strand to one of the wrapped loops. Then individually crimp each of the tails at one end of the braid to the same loop (**photo a**). Use a hemostat to secure the carnelian strand.

7. Thread the unattached end of the carnelian strand through the donut from front to back and the braid through the donut from back to front (**photo b**). Center the donut.

8. Tighten the beads and crimp the carnelian strand to the other wrapped loop. Then crimp the three tails at the end of the braid to the same wrapped loop, as in step 6.

9. Thread one of the wires through the cone from the wide end. String a 5 x 8mm silver bead on the wire to finish the end of the cone. Pull the wire up so it fits snugly and begin a wrapped loop above the silver bead (**photo c**). Thread one ring of the clasp into the loop before completing the wrap. Repeat this step with the other wire, cone, and clasp ring.

— *Louise Malcolm*

materials
necklace 21 in. (.53m)
- 16-in. (41cm) strand 13mm box-shaped carnelians
- 16-in. (41cm) strand 6mm green jade
- 2 16-in. (41cm) strands 2.5 x 4mm amber disks
- 55mm stone donut with a 30mm hole (Eclectica, 262-641-0910, eclecticabeads.com)
- 2 30mm sterling silver cones
- 40-50 1.5mm sterling spacers
- 2 5 x 8mm Bali silver beads
- 2g seed beads, size 11º to match amber
- 2g seed beads, size 11º to match jade
- 8 ft. (2.4m) flexible beading wire, .012–.014
- 10 tube-style crimp beads
- 8 in. (20cm) sterling silver wire, half-hard, 18–20-gauge
- S-hook clasp with two soldered jump rings

Tools: wire cutters, roundnose and chainnose pliers, hemostats

EDITOR'S NOTE: A hemostat is a small clamp used by surgeons. It is often available at beading and craft stores, or may be found at medical supply stores. Other types of beading clamps can be substituted.

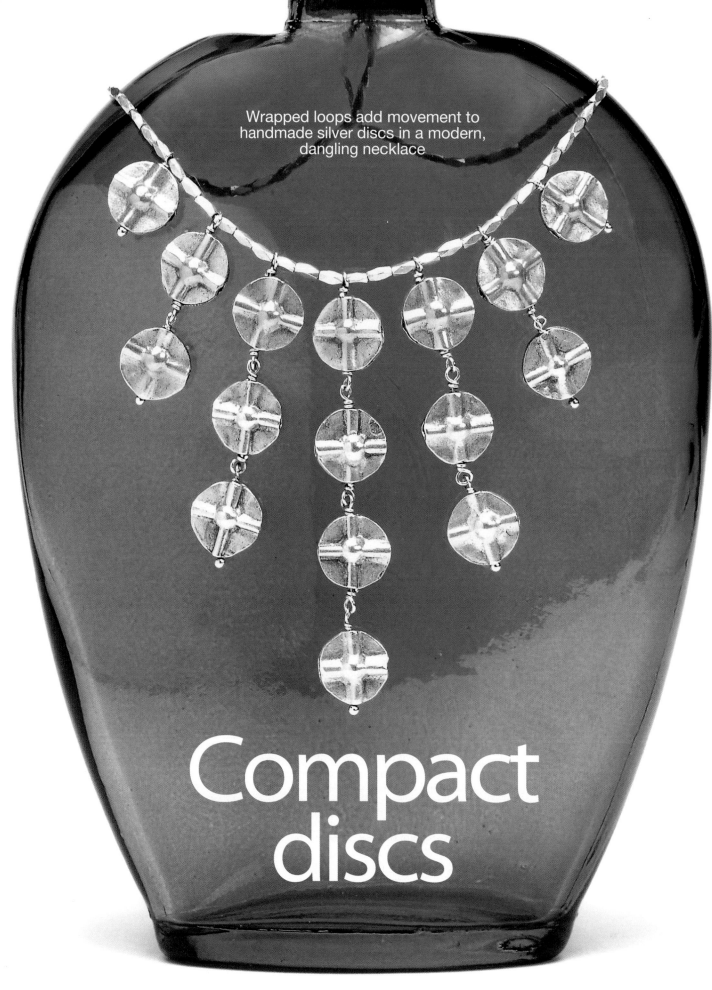

Wrapped loops add movement to handmade silver discs in a modern, dangling necklace

Compact discs

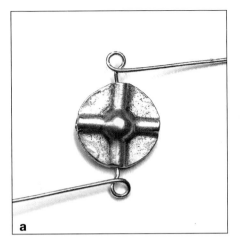

a

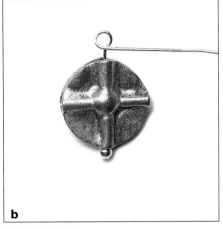

b

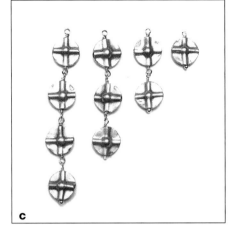

c

materials

necklace 14 in. (36cm)

- **16** 12mm silver disc beads
- 16-in. (41cm) 2 x 4mm silver faceted beads
- 27 in. (69cm) 22-gauge sterling silver wire
- **7** 2-in. (5cm) decorative silver head pins
- flexible beading wire, .014 or .015
- silver toggle clasp
- **2** silver crimp beads

Tools: chainnose and roundnose pliers, diagonal wire cutters, crimping pliers (optional)

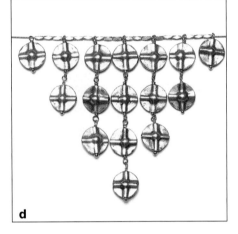

d

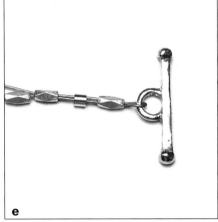

e

1. Cut nine 3-in. (7.6cm) pieces of 22-gauge wire. On each piece, string a disc and make the first half of a wrapped loop on each end (**photo a** and Basics, p. 8).

2. String a disc on each head pin and make the first half of a wrapped loop (**photo b**).

3. Make a four-disc dangle by linking three discs from step 1 with a disc from step 2. Make two three-disc dangles by linking two discs from step 1 with a disc from step 2. Make two two-disc dangles by linking a disc from step 1 with a disc from step 2. Complete the wraps on all loops. Make two single dangles by completing the wraps on the remaining discs (**photo c**).

4. Determine the finished length of your necklace. (This one is 14 in./36cm.)

Add 6 in. (15cm) and cut a piece of flexible beading wire to that length. Center the four-disc dangle on the wire. On each side of the center dangle, string three faceted silver beads, a three-disc dangle, three beads, a two-disc dangle, three beads, and a single dangle (**photo d**).

5. On each end, string approximately 5 in. (13cm) of faceted beads, a crimp bead, a faceted bead, and half the clasp. Go back through the faceted bead, crimp bead, and one more bead (**photo e**). Tighten the wire, check the fit, and add or remove beads, if necessary. Crimp the crimp beads (Basics) and trim the excess wire. Repeat on the other end.

— *Naomi Fujimoto*

Gemstone garland

Combine faceted gemstones
with rings of briolettes and a
beautiful art bead

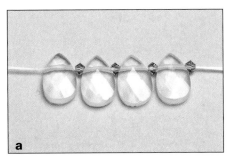

materials

necklace 17 in./.43m

- 20-30mm focal bead
- **12** 15–25mm gemstone nuggets
- **6** 8mm round gemstones
- **6-10** 6mm faceted rondelles
- **30** 8 x 12mm briolettes or teardrop beads
- **36-42** 2mm round beads or 3mm Swarovski bicone crystals
- flexible beading wire, .018–.019
- Nymo B or D beading thread or Fireline fishing line, 6 lb. test
- beading needles, #12 or 13
- G-S Hypo Cement
- **2** crimp beads
- clasp (p. 26, pacificsilverworks.com)

Tools: crimping pliers, diagonal wire cutters

1. Working with a 12-in. (30cm) length of Nymo doubled or a single length of Fireline, string a briolette and a 3mm bead or crystal four times (**photo a**).

2. Tie the working thread and tail together with a square knot (Basics, p. 8 and **photo b**). Sew through the beads again in the same direction.

3. Secure the threads with a second square knot, dab the knot with glue, and sew through the next bead on the ring. Thread a needle on the tail and sew through the next bead on the ring in the opposite direction. Trim the threads and glue the ends inside the bead.

4. Make a total of six bead rings following steps 1-3.

5. Cut a piece of flexible beading wire 4 in. (10cm) longer than the desired finished length of the necklace (this one is 17 in./43cm including the clasp).

6. String the focal bead to the center of the wire. Then string a briolette ring, a 6mm bead, and a rondelle on each side of the focal bead. If the briolette ring doesn't stay centered around the 6mm

bead, string a 3mm bead before the briolette ring and string the ring over it (**photo c**).

7. On each end of the necklace, string a gemstone nugget, a 3mm bead, a briolette, a 3mm bead, a nugget, a rondelle, a 6mm bead, and a briolette ring (**photo d**). Remember to string a 3mm bead before the briolette ring as in the previous step.

8. Continue stringing the pattern from step 7 on both ends of the necklace until the necklace is the desired length.

9. To attach the clasp, string a crimp bead, go through the loop on the clasp, and back through the crimp bead and the bead before it (**photo e**).

10. Crimp the crimp bead (Basics) and trim the excess wire. Repeat on the other end of the necklace with the remaining clasp section. Tighten the wire before crimping.

— *Juana Jelen*

Coast to coast

Create a bright, dramatic necklace using a focal bead of carved borosilicate glass

1. Cut four 24-in. (61cm) lengths of flexible beading wire. String a crimp bead to the center of the four wires.

2. Crimp the crimp bead (Basics, p. 8). Since the wires are fine, give the crimp bead an extra squeeze with chainnose pliers (**photo a**).

3. String a wood barrel bead over all four wires on each side of the crimp bead. Then string the focal bead over the crimp and wood beads (**photo b**). You may need to string another bead or two to fill the focal bead.

4. Working one side of the necklace at a time, string two Charlottes, then a random pattern of beads on each strand (**photo c**) for approximately 8 in. (20cm).

5. Push the beads on each strand against the focal bead (**photo d**). A few of the Charlottes will slide into the focal bead's hole.

6. String two to three Charlottes on each strand. Then string a 6mm bead, a crimp bead, and a 6mm bead. Pass the wire ends through the loop on half the clasp, then go back through the 6mm beads and the crimp (**photo e**).

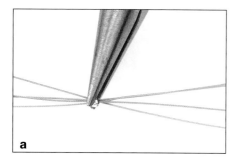

a

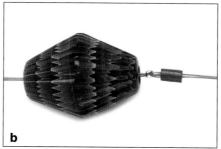

b

c

EDITOR'S NOTE: The 2005 Bead&Button show commemorative bead by Jared DeLong of Lost Coast Art Glass and Gallery is carved borosilicate glass. If you can't find a show bead, you can substitute another bead by Jared or a similar art bead.

materials

necklace 19 in. (.5m)

- 25mm focal bead
  (2005 Bead&Button Show bead,
  800-554-0197, or Lost Coast Art
  Glass, 707-677-0717,
  hotglass@reninet.com)
- 2 16-in. (41cm) strands 4mm
  faceted rondelle stones
- 2 16-in. strands 2–3mm round
  amber or glass beads
- 16-in. strand 4mm wood
  barrel beads
- 5g Charlottes, size 13º
- 4 6mm round beads
- flexible beading wire, size .010
- Nymo D
- beading needles, #13
- **3** crimp beads
- clasp

Tools: crimping pliers, wire cutters, chainnose pliers (optional)

7. Crimp the crimp bead and trim the excess wires.

8. Repeat steps 4–7 to finish the other side of the necklace.

9. Thread a needle with a 10-in. (25 cm) length of Nymo and pick up 15 Charlottes. Working next to the focal bead, tie the tail and the working thread together around all four strands with a square knot (Basics and **photo f**).

10. Go through the Charlottes again. Secure the working thread and tail with half-hitch knots (Basics) between a few beads. Trim the tails.

11. Repeat steps 9–10 on the other side of the focal bead.

— *Cheryl Phelan*

d

e

f

Dichroic glass pendants create
a lively, adjustable necklace

Delicate dichro

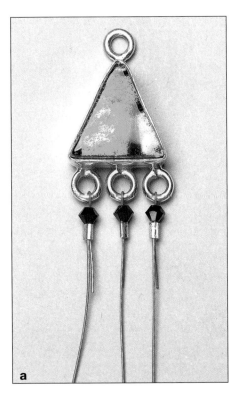

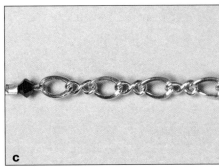

String three strands

Liquid silver is another name for sterling silver bugle beads.

1. Cut three 12-in. (30cm) strands of beading wire.

2. String a crimp bead and a crystal on one strand. Go through one of the three loops on a connector. Go back through the crystal and crimp bead, tighten the wire, and crimp the crimp bead (Basics, p. 8). Repeat for the other two strands (**photo a**). Trim the wire close to the crimps.

3. String the top strand as follows: nine liquid silvers, one crystal, one dichro, and one crystal (**photo b**). Repeat twice. End with nine liquid silvers and secure the end with tape or hemostats.

4. Middle strand: string six liquid silvers, a crystal, a dichro, and a crystal. Then string nine liquid silvers, a crystal, a dichro, and a crystal three times. Finish with a crystal, a dichro, a crystal, and six liquid silvers. Secure the end.

5. Bottom strand: string five liquid silvers, a crystal, a dichro, and a crystal. String nine liquid silvers, a crystal, a dichro, and a crystal three times. End with five liquid silvers. Secure the end.

6. Repeat step 2, attaching each strand to the corresponding loop on the second connector.

Finish the ends

1. Cut two 12-in. lengths of flexible beading wire.

2. String one wire with a crimp bead and a crystal and go through the single loop on the connector finding. Go back through the crystal and the crimp bead, then crimp.

3. String five liquid silvers and a crystal. Repeat seven times. End with five liquid silvers, a crimp bead, and a crystal.

4. Go through the ring on a lobster clasp and back through the crystal and the crimp bead. Tighten the wire and crimp the crimp bead.

5. Repeat steps 2 and 3 with the remaining wire and the other end of the necklace.

6. Substitute 2 in. (5cm) of chain for the jump ring and repeat step 4 (**photo c**). Feel free to use chain scraps here as long as the links are large enough for your clasp.

7. To finish the chain, string a crystal, a seed bead, and a crystal on a plain or ball head pin. Make the first half of a wrapped loop (Basics) above the beads. Attach the loop to the end chain link and finish the wraps (**photo d**).

— *Irina Miech*

materials
necklace 16–18 in. (.41-.46m)

- 2 3-1 dichroic glass connector findings and **12** 8mm dichroic glass pendants (Eclectica, 262-641-0910, eclecticabeads.com)
- **51** 3mm Swarovski bicones, or fire-polished Czech glass beads
- ½ oz. liquid silver twist (Rio Grande, 800-545-6566, riogrande.com)
- flexible beading wire, .010
- **10** silver micro crimps
- lobster clasp
- 2-in. (51mm) chain, links large enough for the lobster clasp
- ball or plain head pin

Tools: chainnose and roundnose pliers, micro crimpers, hemostats (optional)

Quartz medallion

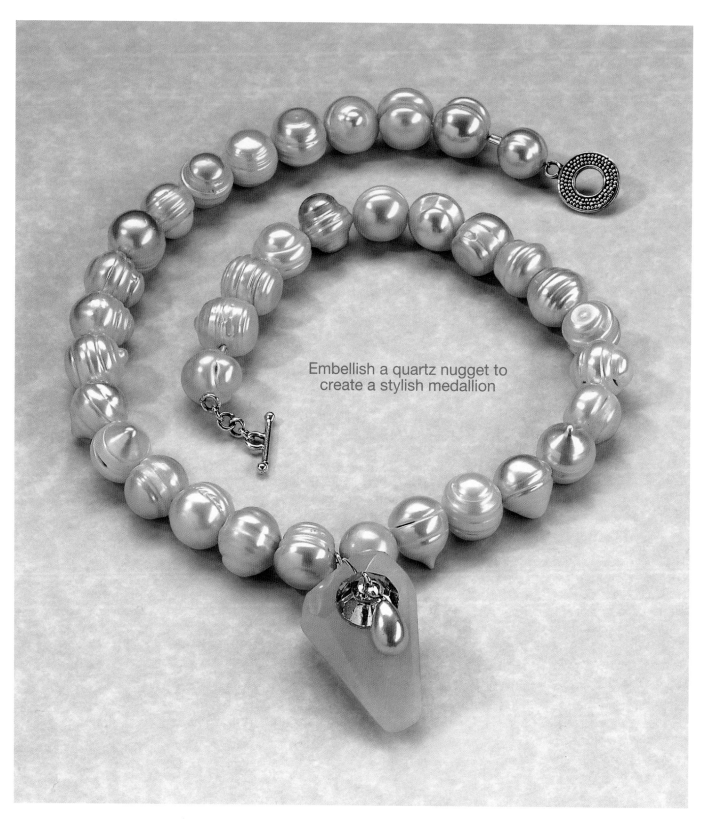

Embellish a quartz nugget to create a stylish medallion

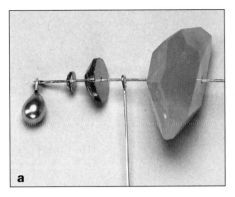

a

b

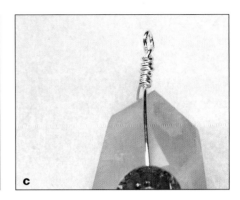

c

d

e

1. Open the loop on an eye pin (Basics, p. 8) and attach a pearl drop or small charm. Close the loop. This is the first eye pin.

2. String a small flat-back crystal, a large flat-back crystal, a second eye pin, and the quartz nugget onto the first eye pin (**photo a**). Slide them against the loop.

3. Bend the tail of the first eye pin up and against the back of the nugget to hold the crystal assembly in place. Hold the second eye pin so the tail points upward and shape it against the curves of the nugget. Wrap the first eye pin's tail around the second one several times as if making a wrapped loop (Basics and **photo b**). Trim the excess wire close to the wraps.

4. Use the wire extending above the nugget to make a wrapped loop about ⅛ in. (3mm) above the wraps made in step 3. Make the wraps from this loop meet the existing wraps (**photo c**). Trim the excess wire.

5. Determine the finished length of your necklace (this one is 16 in./40cm), add 6 in. (15cm), and cut a piece of beading wire to that length. Center the medallion on the wire.

6. String pearls on both ends of the necklace (**photo d**) until you are about 3 in. (7.6cm) from the desired length. Check the fit.

7. String a spacer bead, a crimp bead, a spacer, and half the clasp on one end of the necklace. Go back through the last beads strung (**photo e**), tighten the wire, and crimp the crimp bead (Basics). Trim the excess wire close to the spacer. Repeat on the other end.

— Brenda Schweder

EDITOR'S NOTE: If you can't find a center-drilled gemstone nugget, substitute a top-drilled nugget of the same size, and make a dangle with a wrapped loop.

materials

necklace 16 in. (.4m)

- 15mm center-drilled quartz or other gemstone nugget
- 10mm flat-back sew-on crystal (Jo-Ann Fabrics or craft stores)
- 16-in. (.4m) strand 10mm round freshwater pearls
- 5mm pearl dangle with loop or other small charm
- 4mm flat-back sew-on crystal
- **4** 3mm round spacer beads
- **2** 3-in. (76mm) eye pins
- **2** crimp beads
- toggle clasp
- flexible beading wire, .014 or .015

Tools: chainnose and roundnose pliers, diagonal wire cutters, crimping pliers (optional)

Pastel potpourri

A delicate blend of gemstone chips
highlights a fringed necklace

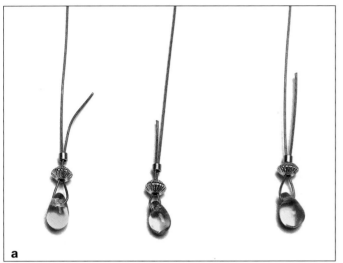

a

b

c

d

e

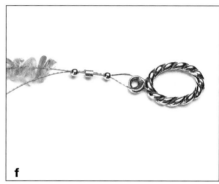

f

1. To make a 20-in. (.5m) necklace, cut one 6-in. (15cm) and two 30-in. (.76m) lengths of beading wire.

2. String a crimp bead, a saucer bead (optional), and an accent bead at the end of each strand. Go back through the beads, tighten the wire, and crimp the crimp bead (**photo a** and Basics, p. 8).

3. String 2 in. (5cm), 2½ in. (6cm), and 3½ in. (9cm) of gemstones on the three strands as shown in **photo b**.

4. String a crimp bead over all three strands (**photo c**).

5. Crimp the crimp bead ½ in. (1.3cm) above the beads. Trim the shortest beading wire ½ in. above the crimp bead (**photo d**).

6. String the focal bead over the strands, hiding the short tail and the crimp bead. Separate the strands and string 8½ in. (21cm) of gemstone chips on each end of the necklace (**photo e**).

7. String a 2mm bead, a crimp bead, a 2mm bead, and the clasp. Go back through these beads (**photo f**). Tighten the wire, but don't crimp the crimp bead. Repeat on the other end. Check the fit and adjust as needed. Crimp the crimp beads and trim the excess wire.

— *Rupa Balachandar*

materials
necklace 20 in. (.5m)
- 20mm silver focal bead
- 2 16-in. (41cm) strands gemstone chip mixture (peridot, amethyst, citrine, aquamarine)
- 3 6mm accent beads
- 3 4mm base metal saucer beads (optional)
- 6 crimp beads
- clasp
- flexible beading wire, .014 or .015
Tools: chainnose or crimping pliers, diagonal wire cutters

Luminosity

Pearls dance with sparkling glass beads and sterling silver in a multistrand necklace

a

b

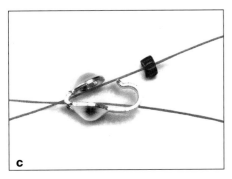

c

d

e

1. Determine the finished length of the inner strand of your necklace. (This inner strand is 16 in./41cm; each subsequent strand is 2½ in./6cm. longer than the previous one.) Add 6 in. (15cm) to the desired length of your inner strand and cut two pieces of Fireline to that length. Repeat, cutting two pieces of Fireline for the middle strands and two for the outer strands. Set aside the pieces cut for the inner and outer strands.

2. Thread a needle on both pieces of Fireline for the middle strand. String a pearl, rondelle, 6mm bead, and rondelle. Repeat, stringing a total of four 6mm beads (**photo a**). String one more pearl and center the beads on the strand.

3. Thread the second needle on the opposite end. String an alternating pattern of rondelles and pearls on each end until the center strand is 1 in. (2.5cm) shorter than the desired length for that strand (**photo b**). Remove the needles.

4. Repeat step 2 on the inner strand, stringing a total of five 6mm beads and ending with a pearl. Thread a second

needle on the opposite end. String two pearls on each end, then string a pattern of one rondelle and three pearls on each end until the inner strand is 1 in. from the desired length for that strand. Remove the needles.

5. Repeat step 2 on the outer strand, stringing a total of five 6mm beads and ending with a pearl. Thread a second needle on the opposite end. String two pearls on each end, then string a pattern of one rondelle and five pearls on each end until the inner strand is 1 in. shorter than the desired length for that strand.

6. String a clamshell bead tip on one end of one of the strands, with the hook end away from the beads. Slide a seed bead on one of the lengths of Fireline (**photo c**).

7. Tie the two ends together using a surgeon's knot (Basics, p. 8). Apply a drop of cement and close the bead tip with chainnose pliers (**photo d**). Let the cement dry, then trim the excess thread. Repeat on each end of each strand, making sure the strands stay flexible.

8. Starting with the center strand, wrap the bead tip's hook around the clasp's

materials
necklace 16 in. (.4m)
- 2 16-in. (41cm) strands 7mm potato-shaped pearls
- **72 or more** 5 x 7mm faceted glass rondelles
- 14 6mm round laser-finished sterling silver beads
- 6 seed beads
- 6 clamshell tips
- 3-strand box clasp
- Fireline, 6 lb. test
- 2 twisted wire needles
- G-S Hypo Cement

Tools: roundnose and chainnose pliers, scissors

center loop (**photo e**). Attach the inner and outer strands to their respective loops. Repeat to attach the opposite ends to the remaining clasp half, keeping the strands in order.

— *Linda Augsburg*

Crystal lace

Combine delicate cylinder beads and
sparkling crystals for an exquisite necklace

String the necklace

1. Begin with 24 in. (61cm) of flexible
beading wire. For the first side, string a
crimp bead and 11 main color (A)
Japanese cylinder beads. Pass the wire
through the crimp to form a loop,
leaving a ½-in. (1.3cm) tail (**photo a**).
Crimp the crimp (Basics, p. 8).

2. String 26 As, sliding them over the
tail of the beading wire. String a color B,
a crystal, and a B.

3. String 26 As, a B, three crystals,
and a B.

4. To string the center, string 26 As, a B,
three As, and a B.

5. String a crystal, a B, four As, and a B.
Repeat this step 11 times for a total of
12 segments.

6. End the center with a crystal, a B,
three As, and a B.

7. String the second side by repeating
step 3, then step 2.

8. String 26 As, a crimp, five As, a
lobster claw and five As. (To use an
S-hook, substitute a bead for the lobster
claw and complete a loop as on the
opposite end.) Slide the end of the wire
back through the crimp and several
more beads. Pull snug, but do not crimp

until the lace portion of the necklace is
complete. Temporarily secure the tail
with tape.

Bead the lace

1. Thread a needle with 2 yd. (1.8m) of
Silamide. Leaving a 12-in. (30cm) tail,
pass the needle through the three As and
one B before the first of the 13 center
crystals (**photo b**). Temporarily secure
the tail with tape.

a

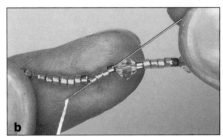

b

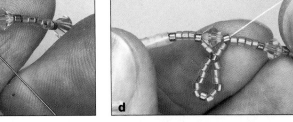

2. String two As, a B, three As, a B, two As, a B, two As, a B, and three As. Pass the needle up through the first B strung (**photo c**) to form a loop.

3. Add two As, then sew through the B after the first crystal (**photo d**).

4. String two As and two crystals. Sew down through the side B of the previous loop (**photo e**) and back up the last crystal strung (**photo f**).

5. Add one crystal and one B. Skip the B and pass the needle through the third and first crystals (**photo g**).

6. String two As, and pass the needle through the B before the next crystal on the beading wire (**photo h**).

7. String two As, a B, three A, pass the needle down through the B that extends from the last crystal strung (**photo i**). String two As, a B, two A, a B, and three A. Pass the needle up through the first B strung in this step to form a loop as in **photo c**.

8. Repeat steps 3-7 for a total of 12 three-crystal clusters, ending with a loop.

9. String two As, then pass the needle through three As and one B after the last center crystal on the beading wire. Add six As and go through the side B on the last loop (**photo j**). Continue through the two As and one B that follow to exit the bottom B of the loop.

10. Add four As, a B, a crystal, a B and four As. Go through the bottom B on the next loop (**photo k**). Repeat this step eleven times for a total of twelve swags across the bottom of the necklace.

11. Finish the lace pattern as it began: go up through one B, two As and one B. Add six As and go through the second B before the first center crystal on the beading wire toward the center.

Finish the necklace

1. Weave the tails into the lace portion of the necklace and tie several half hitch knots (Basics) between beads.

2. Snug all the beads along the flexible beading wire and crimp the remaining crimp bead.

— *Anna Nehs*

materials
necklace 16½ in. (41.9cm)
- 72 4mm bicone Austrian crystals
- 7.5g Japanese cylinder beads (Delicas), size 11º, A color
- 2g Japanese cylinder beads, size 11º, B color
- flexible beading wire, .012–.015
- Silamide to match bead color
- beading needles, #12
- lobster claw clasp
- 2 crimp beads

Tools: crimping pliers, wire cutters

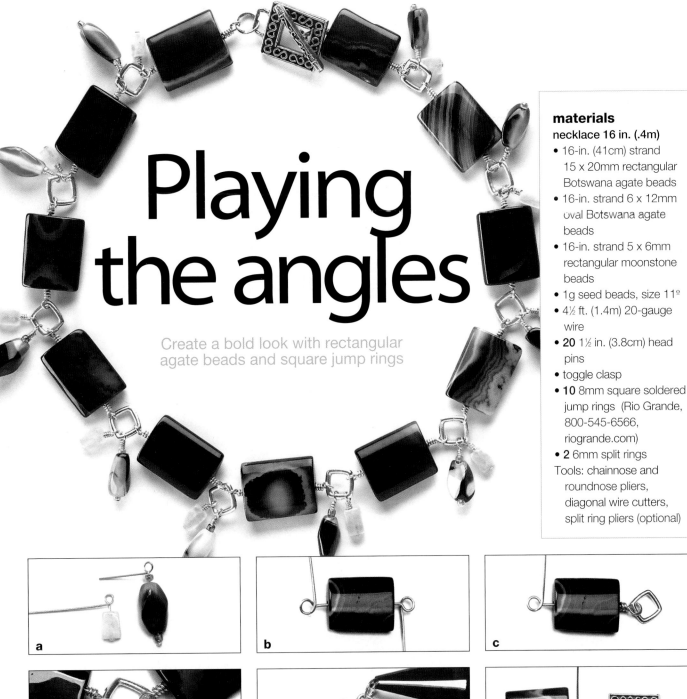

Playing the angles

Create a bold look with rectangular agate beads and square jump rings

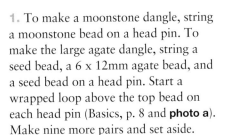

a

b

c

d

e

f

1. To make a moonstone dangle, string a moonstone bead on a head pin. To make the large agate dangle, string a seed bead, a 6 x 12mm agate bead, and a seed bead on a head pin. Start a wrapped loop above the top bead on each head pin (Basics, p. 8 and **photo a**). Make nine more pairs and set aside.
2. Cut a 4½-in. (11cm) piece of wire. Make the first half of a wrapped loop at one end, string a 15 x 20mm agate, and

start another wrapped loop (**photo b**).
3. Slide a square jump ring into a loop and finish the wraps (**photo c**). Make ten or more components, depending on the desired length. (This one is 16 in. /41cm.)
4. Link the units by sliding the jump ring of one unit into the next unit's open loop. Complete the wraps. Make one more unit, omitting the jump ring, and attach it as the end unit.
5. On the lower corner of each jump

ring, attach one pair of dangles. Complete the wraps (**photo d**).
6. Open a split ring (Basics) and slide it on one half of the clasp (**photo e**). Repeat with the remaining clasp half.
7. Slide each split ring on an end loop and complete the wraps (**photo f**).

— *Paulette Biedenbender*

41

Link faceted rondelles for a silk
flower-adorned choker

Floral fantasy

a

b

c

1. Make sure the layers of the flower are
well attached and glued together
or glue the layers together and let dry.
Cut the stem from the flower.
2. Using needle and thread, sew the five-
hole spacer bar to the back of the flower
through the end holes (**photo a**). Be sure
to sew through several layers of petals.
3. Cut a 2½-in. (6cm) length of wire.
Make the first half of a wrapped loop
(Basics, p. 8) on one end. Slide a jump
ring onto the loop and complete the
wraps. Insert the wire into the hole at
one end of the spacer bar (**photo b**).

4. Make the first half of a wrapped
loop ⅛ in. (3mm) from the bar. Slide a
jump ring onto the loop as before and
complete the wraps, ending the wraps as
close to the bar as possible (**photo c**).
5. Cut a 2½-in. length of wire. Start a
wrapped loop and connect the loop
to one of the jump rings (**photo d**).
Complete the wrapped loop with three
to four wraps.
6. Slide a rondelle on the wire. Start
a wrapped loop ⅛ in. beyond the
rondelle. Slide a jump ring onto the loop
(**photo e**). Complete the loop with three

to four wraps. The rondelle should
nestle snugly between the wraps.
7. Repeat steps 5 (**photo f**) and 6 on
each side of the spacer bar until your
necklace is about 2 in. (5cm) short of
the desired length. Keep the flower off-
center. This necklace measures 15 in.
(38cm) from the clasp to the first link of
the chain extender and has 10 rondelle
units on one side and six on the other.
8. Repeat steps 3–7 in the center and
end holes of the spacer bar. Since this is
a choker, keep the wrapped rondelle
units consistent in length and number.

materials

necklace 15 in. (38cm)

- silk flower
- **49** 5 x 8mm faceted glass rondelles
- **12** 2.5mm round gold-filled beads
- **3** five-hole 27mm spacer bars
- **54** 4mm soldered jump rings
- **13 ft.** (4m) 22-gauge half-hard, gold-filled wire
- 2½ in. (6cm) piece of chain
- **5** 2-in. (5cm) head pins
- lobster claw clasp
- glue (optional)

Tools: roundnose and chainnose pliers, diagonal wire cutters, utility cutters, bent chainnose pliers (optional), sewing needle, scissors, and thread

d

e

f

g

h

i

j

9. At one end, string a 2.5mm bead, the end hole of a spacer bar, and a 2.5mm bead on a head pin. Start a wrapped loop ⅛ in. from the bead, slide the jump ring from one outer strand onto the loop, and complete the wraps. Repeat with the other outer strand and go through the hole on the opposite end of the spacer bar (**photo g**).

10. To finish the center strand, cut a 2½-in. piece of wire and start a wrapped loop. Slide the jump ring from the center strand onto the loop and complete the wraps. String a 2.5mm bead, the center

hole of the spacer bar, and a 2.5mm bead on the wire (**photo h**).

11. Start a wrapped loop ⅛ in. from the 2.5mm bead. Slide one end of the chain onto the loop and complete the wraps. The chain makes the necklace adjustable. String a rondelle on a head pin. Start a wrapped loop ⅛ in. from the rondelle. Slide the end link of chain into the loop and complete the wraps (**photo i**).

12. Repeat steps 9 and 10 on the other end of the necklace. Make the first part of a wrapped loop ⅛ in. from the 2.5mm

bead. Slide the lobster claw clasp onto the loop and finish the wraps (**photo j**).

— *Linda Augsburg*

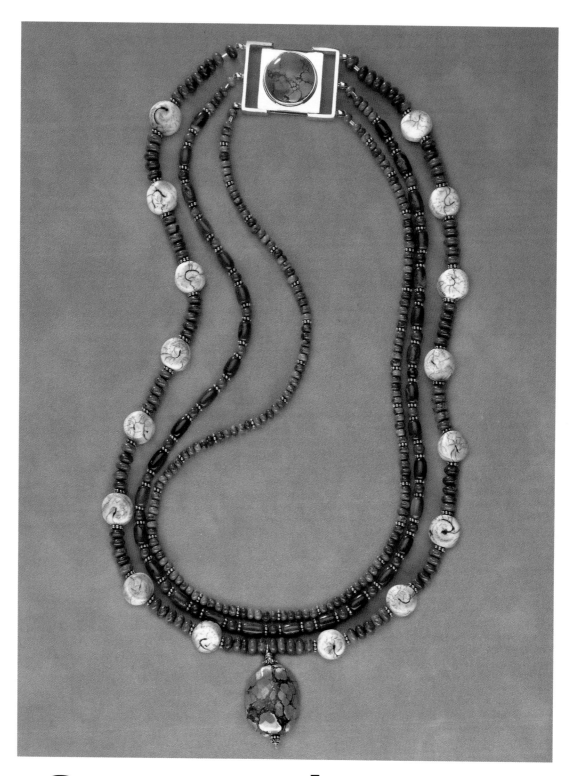

Stone shapes and shells

1. Determine the finished length of the first strand of your necklace and subtract the length of the clasp (This one is 19 in./48cm). Cut a length of beading wire 5 in. (13cm) longer than the determined length.

2. String a pattern of five 4mm turquoise rondelles and a 4mm flat silver spacer until you reach the desired length.

3. Cut a second length of beading wire 1 in. (2.5cm) longer than the first. String a pattern of a barrel stone, a 4mm spacer, a round stone, and a silver spacer. Repeat until the strand is an inch longer than the previous strand.

4. Cut a third length of beading wire 2 in. (5cm) longer than the second and string 2 in. more of beads in the following pattern: five 6mm rondelles, a 4mm spacer, a shell, and a spacer. At the center of the strand string ten rondelles between two spacers and then continue the pattern for the remaining half of the strand. You'll add a pendant later.

5. Hold the 4-in. (10cm) length of wire in your non-dominant hand and place one end on the anvil. Flatten the end with a hammer (**photo a**) until the decorative silver spacer won't fall off the wire. File any rough edges. If the hole of the spacer is large and it slides off the wire, stop hammering — the wire will become brittle. Trim the flattened end from the wire. Use chainnose pliers to

make a small hook at the tip of the wire and pinch it closed with the pliers, or make a small loop (Basics, p. 8) instead.

6. String the large stone on the wire above the silver spacer and string a second spacer. Make the first half of a wrapped loop (Basics and **photo b**).

7. Slide the loop onto the beading wire at the center of the third strand so there are 5 stones on each side of the pendant (**photo c**). Complete the wrap and trim the wire.

8. Check the length of each strand and add or remove beads as necessary. String a crimp bead and a rondelle on one end of the first strand. Pass the wire through a loop on the clasp, back through the last rondelle, the crimp bead, and a few more stones (**photo d**). Crimp the crimp bead (Basics) and trim the tail. Repeat with the unfinished end and the other clasp half.

9. Repeat step 8 with the remaining strands. Carefully try on the necklace to check the length before crimping the last 2 strands.

— *Cheryl Phelan*

materials
(necklace 24 in. (.61m))

- faceted turquoise stone (approx. 25mm)
- **16** 12mm round shell beads (Kamol, 206-764-7375)
- 18-in. (46cm) strand 6mm turquoise rondelles
- **2** 16-in. (41cm) strands 4mm turquoise rondelles
- 18-in. strand 4mm turquoise round beads and 7mm barrels
- **129** 4mm sterling silver flat spacers
- 4 in. (10cm) 22-gauge sterling silver wire, half-hard
- **2** decorative silver spacers
- flexible beading wire, size .014
- **6** crimp beads
- 3-strand clasp (Natural Touch Beads, 707-935-7049)

Tools: chainnose and roundnose pliers, wire cutter, crimping pliers, anvil, hammer, metal file, multi-strand bead design board (optional)

Quartz complement

Combine intricate carved quartz with classic cloisonné

a

b

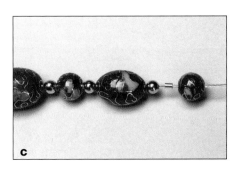

c

Carved quartz beads showcase intricate craftsmanship but carry meager price tags. Together, two large quartz beads cost about $15. Combine them with cloisonné and braids of small quartz beads and you have a stylish yet inexpensive necklace. To alter the look, substitute gemstones for the cloisonné.

1. Cut your beading wire into three 36-in. (.9m) pieces. Center one 18 x 12mm bead on all three wires. Clamp or tape the wires on one side of the bead.
2. String a spacer, an 8mm round, a spacer, and a carved quartz bead (**photo a**). String a spacer, an 8mm round, a spacer, an 18 x 12mm bead, a spacer, an 8mm round, a spacer, a 15 x 10mm oval, and a spacer (**photo b**).
3. String a 1mm crimp bead and an 8mm round on the three wires (**photo c**). Snug the beads, crimp the crimp bead (Basics, p. 8), then slide the 8mm round over the crimp.
4. String 35 round quartz beads on each of the three wires, taping the ends to keep the beads snug. Braid the three tails as shown in the **figure** and **photo d**. Remove the tape.
5. String one 1mm crimp on the three wires, then snug it up to the beads. Crimp the crimp bead. String an 8mm round over the crimp. String one 2mm

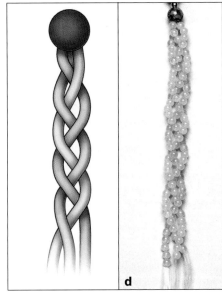

d

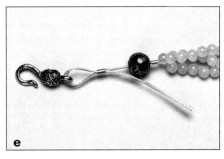

e

crimp and the clasp's loop. Go back through the 2mm crimp (**photo e**). Tape the three tails together, if necessary for easier threading. Tighten the beads, crimp the crimp bead, then cut the tails.
6. Repeat steps 2–5 on the other side of the center bead to complete the necklace.

— *Dawn Hardy*

materials
- 2 45 x 13mm carved melon rose quartz beads (Fire Mountain Gems, 800-355-2137, firemountaingems.com)
- 3 18 x 12mm oval cloisonné beads or moss agate gemstones
- 2 15 x 10mm oval cloisonné beads or rose quartz gemstones
- 10 8mm round cloisonné beads or lapidolite gemstones
- 210 4mm round rose quartz gemstones
- 10 4mm round spacers
- 4 1mm crimps
- 2 2mm crimps
- S-hook and soldered jump ring on hook-and-eye clasp
- 9 ft. (2.8m) flexible beading wire, .012–.014
Tools: wire cutters, crimping pliers, hemostats (optional)

Knotty and nice

Enjoy a glimpse of colorful thread in this knotted pearl necklace

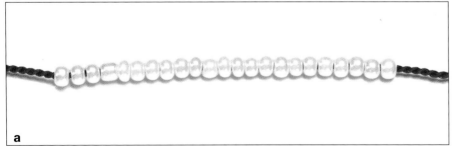

a

EDITOR'S NOTE: You can use crimp covers instead of bead tips to cover the knots at the ends of this necklace.

1. String enough seed beads to create a loop that your button or bead will fit snugly through (**photo a**). Slide the seed beads to the end of the bead cord. Make a perfection loop (see p. 49), using the beaded portion as your second loop. Glue the knot and trim the tail.
2. Cut the loop off a bead tip and slide it (open end first) on the thread and over the knot. Close the bead tip with chainnose pliers (**photo b**).
3. String all the pearls on the thread and slide them to the needle end (**photo c**).

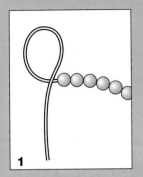
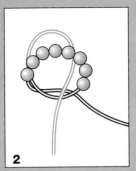
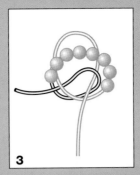
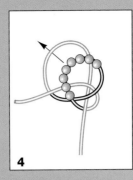
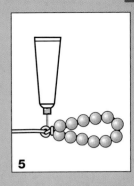

Perfection loop

1. Form a single loop by bringing the beaded tail behind the working cord. Keep this tail on the right-hand side.

2. Make a smaller loop in front of the first by bringing the beaded tail around the first loop. End with the tail on the right. Hold the loops as shown.

3. Bring the tail between the two loops and hold it on the left-hand side.

4. Pull the beaded loop through the first loop as shown. Make sure the tail does not slip and tighten the knot.

5. Trim the tail close to the knot and dab the knot with glue.

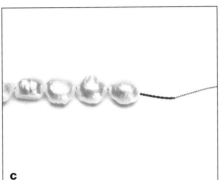
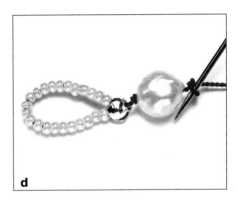
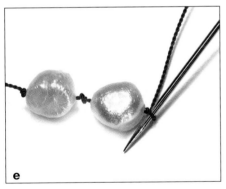

4. Make an overhand knot (Basics, p. 8) and use the pin or awl to slide it next to the bead tip. Slide a pearl next to the knot. Make an overhand knot and slide it next to the pearl (**photo d**). Continue knotting the pearls until the necklace is the desired length (**photo e**). End the pearl section with a knot.

5. Trim the end off the second bead tip and string it next to the last knot (hinged end first). String the large bead or button and a seed bead. Go back through the bead or button (**photo f**).

6. Make two half-hitch knots (Basics) under the bead or button. Glue the knots, trim the ends, and close the bead tip (**photo g**). (It won't cover the knot, but provides symmetry with the other end.) Leave enough slack to slide the button through the loop.

— *Karin Buckingham*

materials
- 16-in. (.41cm) strand 8mm freshwater pearls
- 1g seed beads, size 11º
- bead or button for clasp, 10–15mm
- 2 clamshell bead tips
- Polyamid bead cord with fixed needle, size 6
- G-S Hypo Cement

Tools: chainnose pliers, diagonal wire cutters, pin or awl

Sand life luxury

Create an earthy yet dramatic look with a glass disc bead

a

b

c

d

e

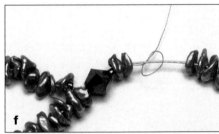

f

g

h

materials

necklace 17-in. (43cm)

- round glass focal bead (Sand Life, Harold Cooney)
- 16-in. (41cm) strand heishi pearls
- 9 6mm crystals, bicone
- 4 3mm silver beads
- 1g Japanese cylinder beads
- 2 crimp beads
- clasp
- 22 in. (.6mm) flexible beading wire, size .012-.014
- 15 in. (38cm) Fireline, 6 lb. test
- G-S Hypo cement

Tools: crimping pliers, wire cutters

1. String the focal bead to the center of a 22-in. (56cm) length of flexible beading wire and a 15-in. (38cm) length of Fireline. Tape the ends of the flexible beading wire to your beading surface.
2. String enough cylinder beads on the Fireline to fill the glass bead (**photo a**).
3. Working on the Fireline, string an inch (2.5cm) of pearls on each side of the glass bead (**photo b**). Bring the strands up and around the bead. The pearls should reach the center point directly above it.
4. String a cylinder bead on each end of the Fireline, then pass both ends through a crystal (**photo c**). Secure the strand ends with tape.
5. Remove the tape from one end of the

flexible beading wire and string a crystal, a cylinder bead, 1¾ in. (4cm) of pearls, a cylinder bead, a crystal, and a cylinder bead. Secure the wire with tape and repeat with the other end (**photo d**).
6. Continue stringing both ends of the necklace until it is the desired length minus the length of the clasp. Keep the glass bead centered.
7. String a cylinder bead, 1¾ in. of pearls, and a cylinder bead on one end of the Fireline. Pass the Fireline through the bottom strand's second crystal, the cylinder bead, and a couple of pearls (**photo e**).
8. Adjust both strands so the beads are snug and tie a half-hitch knot (Basics, p. 8) around the flexible

beading wire (**photo f**). Go through a few pearls and tie a second knot. Repeat a few more times and dab the last knots with glue. Trim the excess Fireline. Repeat on the other end.
9. String a silver bead, a crimp, and a silver bead on one end of the necklace. Go through the loop on one of the clasp components and back through the crimp and silver beads (**photo g**).
10. Adjust the tension on this side of the necklace so the beads are snug. Crimp the crimp bead (Basics and **photo h**). Trim the wire and repeat on the other end.

— *Cheryl Phelan*

Graceful curves

Repeat one shape to create
a simple but distinctive necklace

a

b

c

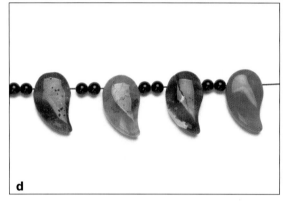

d

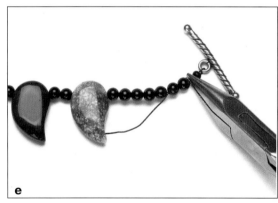

e

1. Determine the finished length of your necklace. (This one is 16½ in./.42m.) Add 6 in. (15cm) and cut a piece of beading wire to that length. String a crimp bead, a seed bead, and one part of the clasp. Go back through the seed bead and the crimp bead (**photo a**).

2. Tighten the wire so it forms a small loop around the clasp and crimp the crimp bead (Basics, p. 8 and **photo b**).

3. String seven 6mm beads and slide them close to the crimp, covering the wire tail (**photo c**). Trim the excess wire.

4. String an alternating pattern of curved beads and round beads until your beaded strand is 1¾ in. (4.4cm) shorter than the desired length (**photo d**).

5. String seven 6mm beads, a crimp bead, a seed bead, and the remaining section of the clasp. Go back through the seed bead, the crimp bead, and a few 6mm beads. Check the fit and add or remove beads as necessary. Tighten the wire, crimp the crimp bead (**photo e**), and trim the excess wire.

—*Candice St. Jacques*

materials
necklace 16½ in. (.42m)
- **20** 20mm curved stone beads
- **50** 6mm round stone beads
- **2** seed beads, size 11º
- flexible beading wire, .019
- **2** crimp beads
- toggle clasp

Tools: chainnose or crimping pliers, wire cutters

Closely linked

Embellish a stamped floral centerpiece with pendants and drops

The components in this necklace are linked with jump rings. Use 3mm jump rings except where the instructions call for the 4mm size.

1. Attach a 12mm drop to a round connector by opening the loop (Basics, p. 8). Repeat with the other drop (**photo a**).

2. Cut two 21-link (1¾ in./ 4.5cm) pieces of chain. Attach each chain to a unit made in step 1 (**photo b**).

3. Attach a square connector to the upper left-hand corner of the stamping with two 4mm jump rings. Repeat on the upper right-hand corner (**photo c**).

4. Attach the 35mm drop to a round connector with a 4mm jump ring (**photo d**).

5. Cut a seven-link (⅝ in./ 1.5cm) piece of chain. Attach the unit made in step 4 to the center link of chain and connect each end of the chain to a loop on the remaining square connector (**photo e**).

6. Attach the square connector to the bottom of the stamping with 4mm jump rings (**photo f**).

7. Connect each chain unit from step 2 to the outer loop on the connectors at the upper corners of the stamping (**photo g**).

8. Attach each rectangular connector to the empty loop on the square connectors (**photo h**).

9. Cut two eight-link (1¹⁄₁₆ in./17mm) pieces of chain. Attach each chain to a rectangular connector. Attach a round connector to the remaining end link of each chain (**photo i**).

10. You can finish the necklace with or without a clasp. To finish without a clasp, cut a length of chain long enough to go over your head. Attach the chain's end links to the round connectors added in step 9.

To finish with a clasp, determine the desired length of chain from the round connector to the clasp. (This

a

b

c

d

e

f

materials

- 21 x 32mm rose-motif stamping (Designer's Findings, 262-574-1324)
- 30 in. (76cm) extra-fine oval link chain
- crystal connectors (Designer's Findings)
  2 5 x 15mm 2-loop rectangles
  5 5mm 2-loop rounds
  3 7mm 4-loop squares
- 35mm pendant drop with loop
- **2** 12mm fat point drops with loop (Designer's Findings)
- **19** 3mm jump rings
- **7** 4mm jump rings
- clasp (optional)

Tools: **2** pairs of pliers (chainnose or bentnose), wire cutters

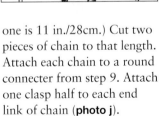

g

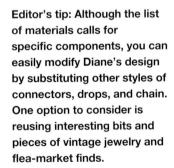

h

i

j

one is 11 in./28cm.) Cut two pieces of chain to that length. Attach each chain to a round connecter from step 9. Attach one clasp half to each end link of chain (**photo j**).

— *Diane Hyde*

Editor's tip: Although the list of materials calls for specific components, you can easily modify Diane's design by substituting other styles of connectors, drops, and chain. One option to consider is reusing interesting bits and pieces of vintage jewelry and flea-market finds.

Formal finery

A sparkling collar with a
dramatic dangle suits the
most special of occasions

1. String a 3mm crystal, the focal bead,
and a 4mm crystal on a head pin. Make
a wrapped loop (Basics, p. 8) above the
top bead (**photo a**).

2. To make the pendant, cut two 7-in.
(18cm) strands of .010 beading wire.
String a 2-in. (5cm) alternating pattern
of 3mm crystals on each strand,
reversing the colors on the second
strand. String a crimp bead over both
wires, then string 1 in. (2.5cm) of
cylinder beads on each strand (**photo b**).

3. String the bottom right wire through
the loop on the dangle and go through
all the crystals on the left. Continue
through the crimp bead and a few
cylinder beads. Repeat with the bottom
left wire, working in the opposite
direction. String the top wires through
the crimp bead and a few crystals,
forming two loops (**photo c**). Tighten the
wires and crimp the crimp bead (Basics).
Trim the excess wire.

a

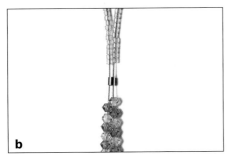

b

c

d

e

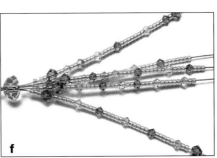

f

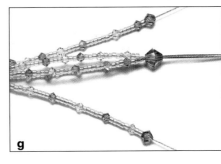

g

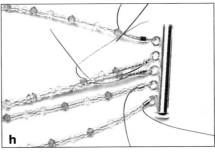

h

4. Determine the finished length of your necklace. (This one is 16 in./41cm.) Add 6 in. (15cm) and cut five pieces of .014 flexible beading wire to that length. String an 8mm crystal rondelle, the pendant, and a rondelle, and center them over all five wires (**photo d**).

5. String three cylinder beads and a 4mm bicone on each wire at one end of the necklace (**photo e**).

6. On each wire, string 2 in. of cylinder beads and 3mm crystals. Vary the placement so the crystals land in different places on the wire (**photo f**).

7. On each outer wire, string a 4mm bicone. String a 6mm bicone over the three middle wires (**photo g**).

8. On each wire, string 6 in. of cylinder beads and 3mm crystals. Vary the placement so the crystals land in different places on the wire.

9. Repeat steps 5–8 on the other end of the necklace.

10. On each wire, string a crimp bead, a cylinder bead, and the respective clasp loop. Go back through the beads just strung and another cylinder bead (**photo h**). Repeat on the other end of the necklace, keeping the clasp in the right orientation.

11. Tighten the wires and check the fit. Add or remove beads if necessary. Crimp the crimp beads and trim the excess wire.

— *Karin Buckingham*

materials
necklace 16 in. (.4m)
- 10mm focal bead
- **2** 8mm crystal rondelles
- **2** 6mm bicone crystals
- **15** 4mm bicone crystals
- **260** bicone 3mm crystals in two colors
- 9g Japanese cylinder beads, size 11º
- **11** crimp beads
- 5-strand slide clasp
- 3-in. (7.6cm) head pin
- flexible beading wire, .014 and .010

Tools: chainnose and roundnose pliers, wire cutters, crimping pliers (optional)

EDITOR'S NOTE: When finishing a multistrand necklace, crimp the middle strand's crimp beads first. Then finish the inner and outer strands, checking the drape and fit of each strand as you work.

Lacy loops

Create a netted collar with delicate loops

Bead the base

1. Pick up one 11º to use as a stop bead and slide it to 12 in. (30cm) from the end of a 3-yd. (2.7m) length of thread. Sew back through the bead in the same direction. Then pick up a color B 11º, three color A 11ºs, a B, three As, a B, three As, a B, and three As. Sew back through the first B strung (**figure 1, a–b**).

2. Pick up three As, a B, three As, a B, and three As. Sew through the last B from the previous step (**b-c**).

3. Repeat step 2 (**c-d**).

4. Repeat until you have about 15½ in. (39cm) of beadwork, ending as in **figure 1, c-d**. This necklace has 39 loops along the edge of the netted base.

5. Pick up three As, a B, and one of the soldered rings. Sew back through the B and three As. Reinforce the clasp and the last inch (2.5cm) of beadwork

with a second thread path (**figure 2, a–b**). Secure the tails with half-hitch knots (Basics, p. 8) between the beads and trim the tail. Leave the other end of the necklace unfinished in case you have to add or remove beads.

Embellish with loops

1. Secure a new 2-yd. (1.8m) length of thread in the beadwork and exit the three As before the bottom B on the first loop (**figure 3, point a**).

2. Pick up six As, a B, and six As. Skip the next edge B and sew through the three As before the next bottom B (**a–b**), then through the existing base beads (**b-c**). Make five loops with the same bead counts.

3. Repeat step 2, picking up seven As, a B, a teardrop bead, and seven As. Make four seven-A loops.

4. Repeat step 2, picking up nine As,

a B, a teardrop bead, a B, and nine As. Make four nine-A loops.

5. Repeat step 2, picking up 11 As, a B, a teardrop bead, a B, and 11 As. Make four 11 A loops.

6. For the center of the necklace, make three loops as above, but use 15 As in the first loop, 17 in the second, and 15 in the third. Make the second half of the necklace to mirror the first. Secure the working thread and trim.

7. Add a jump ring to the other end of the necklace (**figure 2, a–b**) using the tail. Attach the S-clasp to the soldered rings.

— *Lois Fetters*

EDITOR'S NOTE: Make a more dramatic necklace by switching the main and accent colors in the loops or by adding gemstones, pearls, or crystals to the loops in place of the teardrop beads.

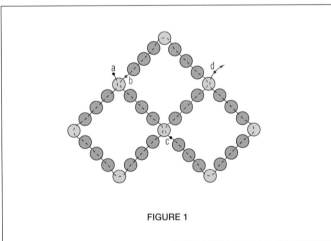

FIGURE 1

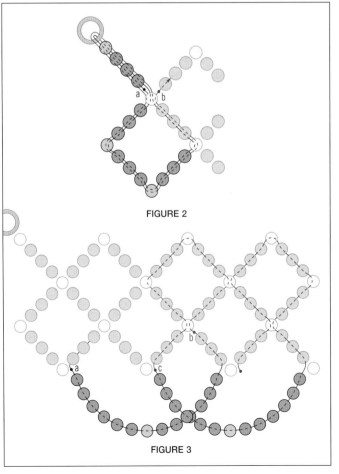

FIGURE 2

FIGURE 3

materials

necklace 16 in. (.41m)

- Japanese seed beads, size 11º
  20g color A
  10g color B
- Japanese 4mm fringe or teardrop beads
- S-clasp with two soldered rings
- Silamide or conditioned Nymo D to match bead color
- beading needles, #12

Working in concert

Compose a harmonious necklace of ribbons,
cords, beads, and spacers

a

b

c

d

e

materials

necklace 20 in. (.5m)

- pendant with loop
- **48–60** assorted beads with holes large enough to accommodate ribbon
- 4g seed beads, size 8º or 6º
- **2** bead caps or cones
- **6 in.** (15cm) 22-gauge wire, half-hard
- **2** multistrand spacer bars
- organza ribbon
- flexible beading wire, size .014
- Mastex or Griffin cord, size 6
- **24** crimp beads (optional)
- clasp
- glue or G-S Hypo Cement

Tools: chainnose and roundnose pliers, diagonal wire cutters, design board or beading surface

1. Determine the finished length of your necklace. (This one is 20 in./51cm.) Add 12 in. (30cm) and cut a total of five strands: three ribbon, one cord, and one beading wire, to that length. Center the pendant over all five strands (**photo a**).

2. Lay the strands and pendant on your design board. Place the spacer bars near the center of each half of the necklace, then arrange your beads. Aim for a random, but balanced, placement of the larger beads.

3. Work on both sides of the pendant at the same time. Thread beads on the ribbons; the thickness of the ribbons should keep the beads in place without knots. Use knots to keep beads in place on the cord. Either string the beading wire solid with beads or use crimp beads on each side of the beads to keep the beads floating on the wire (**photo b**). String each strand through one hole of the spacer bar, adding a bead just

before the bar, if necessary, to keep the strands in place.

4. Continue stringing on each end beyond the spacer bars until the necklace is the desired length. Knot all strands together in an overhand knot (Basics, p. 8), leaving about an inch (2.5cm) from the last beads to the knot. Cut a 3-in. (7.6cm) piece of wire and make the first half of a wrapped loop (Basics). Slide the knot onto the loop (**photo c**). Complete the wraps and trim the wire. Flatten the loop, if necessary, so it will fit into the cone or cap along with the knot. Test the knot, tightening any loose strands.

5. On one end, add a dot of glue or cement on the knot, saturating the ribbons and cords (**photo d**). Let dry. Test to make sure all strands are secure. Trim the strands close to the knot.

6. String the cone on the wire, hiding the knot, ends, and wrapped loop in the

cone. Make the first part of a wrapped loop. String one loop of the clasp onto the wrapped loop. Complete the wraps (**photo e**).

7. Repeat steps 5 and 6 on the other end.

— *Stacey Neilson*

EDITOR'S NOTE: There are two easy ways to thread beads on organza ribbon. One method is to use sharp scissors to cut away the ribbon on one bound edge, cutting diagonally across the ribbon, and using the bound edge as a needle (**photo f**). The second way is to create a harness by folding the end of the ribbon over the center of a piece of flexible beading wire, then folding the wire in half (**photo g**).

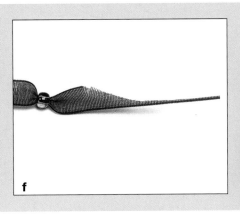

f

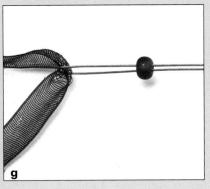

g

Front & center

Turn a clasp into a creative centerpiece

a

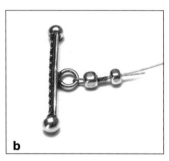

b

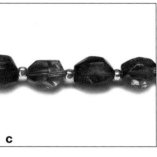

c

d

Amethyst necklace
1. Use roundnose pliers to turn a decorative spiral at one end of the 20-gauge wire or use a purchased head pin. String a nugget. Make the first half of a wrapped loop (Basics, p. 8) above the nugget and connect the loop to the round clasp half (**photo a**). Finish the wraps.
2. Determine the finished length of your necklace. (This one is 19½ in./50cm) Add 6 in. (15cm) and cut a piece of beading wire to that length. String a silver bead, a crimp bead, a silver bead, and the bar end of the clasp. Go

back through the beads (**photo b**). Tighten the wire around the loop and crimp the crimp bead (Basics).
3. String an alternating pattern of nuggets and silver beads until the necklace is 1 in. (2.5cm) shorter than the desired length. End with a silver bead (**photo c**).
4. String a crimp bead, a silver bead, and the loop end of the clasp. Go back through the silver bead, the crimp bead, and several adjacent beads. Tighten the wire and crimp the crimp bead (**photo d**). Trim the excess wire.

materials

**Amethyst necklace
19½ in. (.49m)**
- 16-in. (41cm) strand
  10–12mm amethyst
  nuggets
- 16-in. strand 2.5mm silver
  cube-shaped beads
- 3 in. (7.6cm) 20-gauge wire
  or decorative head pin
- **2** crimp beads
- toggle clasp
- flexible beading wire, .015

Aqua necklace 17 in.(.43m)
- 20mm or larger focal bead
- **31** 6mm mother-of-pearl
  mosaic beads (Eclectica,
  262-641-0910)
- 16-in. strand 4mm brass
  heishi beads
- 1½-in. (4cm) head pin
- 3 in. 20-gauge gold-filled
  wire
- hook-and-eye clasp
- **2** crimp beads
- flexible beading wire, .015

Tools: roundnose and
chainnose pliers, crimping
pliers (optional), wire
cutters

a

b

c

d

e

Aqua necklace

1. String a brass bead, a
mosaic bead, and a brass
bead on a head pin. Make a
wrapped loop (**photo a, left**).
2. Slide a brass bead and the
focal bead on a 3-in. (7.6cm)
length of wire. Make the first
half of a wrapped loop on
both ends (**photo a, right**).
3. Slide the mosaic bead unit
on one of the loops and
finish the wraps. Attach the
unfinished loop to the eye
end of the clasp (**photo b**).
Finish the wraps.
4. Determine the finished
length of your necklace. (This
one is 17 in./43cm.) Add 6 in.
(15cm) and cut a piece of
beading wire to that length.

String a mosaic bead, a crimp
bead, a mosaic bead, and the
hook end of the clasp and go
back through the beads
(**photo c**). Tighten the wire
and crimp the crimp bead.
5. String a pattern of seven
brass beads, a mosaic bead,
a brass bead, and a mosaic
bead until the necklace is
1 in. (2.5cm) shorter than the
desired length. End with
seven brass beads (**photo d**).
6. String a mosaic bead, a
crimp bead, a mosaic bead,
and the remaining clasp

section. Go back through the
mosaic bead, the crimp bead,
and several adjacent beads.
Tighten the wire and crimp
the crimp bead. Trim the
excess wire (**photo e**).

— *Linda Augsburg*

**EDITOR'S NOTE: This
necklace is a great way to
showcase a beautiful clasp.
Since your crimp beads and
beading wire will show, make
sure they match the other
metals in your necklace.**

Chapter 2
Bracelets &Earrings

Mixed metals

Combine rhinestones with lengths of gold and silver chain for a luxe bracelet

a

b

c

d

MATERIALS

bracelet 8 in. (20cm)

- **20** assorted 4- or 5-in. (10–13cm) chain segments, gold and silver
- **4½** ft. (1.4m) 22- or 24-gauge wire, gold-filled
- **10** 4–6mm two-hole rhinestone findings
- **20** 5mm gold jump rings
- 5-strand slide clasp, gold-filled

Tools: chainnose and roundnose pliers, wire cutters

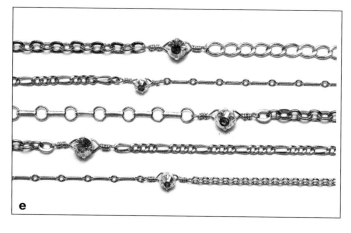

e

f

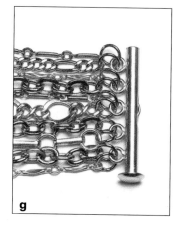

g

1. Cut 20 2½-in. (6cm) pieces of wire. Center a rhinestone finding on two wires. Bend the wires toward each other, then bend one wire upward to form a stem (**photo a**).

2. Wrap the other wire around the stem as if completing a wrapped loop (Basics, p. 8) and trim the excess wire (**photo b**).

3. Make the first half of a wrapped loop with the wire stem, keeping the loop perpendicular to the finding (**photo c**). Attach the loop to the end link of a chain segment and complete the wraps (**photo d**).

4. Repeat steps 2 and 3 with the wires at the other end of the finding and attach another chain segment.

5. Make wrapped-loop components to connect pairs of remaining chain segments. Pair bar-and-link chain segments with cable segments so that you'll have more flexibility when determining the length of each strand. Arrange the ten strands, staggering the placement of the rhinestones across your wrist (**photo e**). Trim the chains so that the strands are the desired length. Cut bar-and-link chains so they end with a round link.

6. Open a jump ring (Basics) and loop it through an end link of chain and a clasp loop. Close the jump ring (**photo f**). Attach the remaining strands in the same way, connecting two strands to each clasp loop (**photo g**). Repeat with the remaining clasp half, making sure to position the clasp correctly. Check the fit and trim the links or add jump rings to lengthen the strands.

— *Naomi Fujimoto*

Make a sophisticated
bracelet and earrings set
with geometric crystals and links

Crystals squared

Bracelet

Crystal links

1. Cut a 1-in. (2.5cm) piece of 20-gauge wire. Make a right-angle bend ⅜ in. (1cm) from one end of the wire with your chainnose pliers.

2. String a crystal against the bend. Make a second right-angle bend below the crystal pointing in the opposite direction from the first (**photo a**).

3. Grasp the tip of the wire with roundnose pliers and turn a small loop (Basics, p. 8). Make a second loop in the same plane as the first (**photo b**).

4. Open a loop (Basics), slide a soldered jump ring into it, and close the loop. Repeat with the remaining loop (**photo c**).

5. Repeat steps 1–4 to make a total of eight crystal links. Connect crystal links to jump rings as in step 4 and end with a jump ring.

Clasp

1. Cut a 3½-in. (9cm) piece of wire and make a 45-degree bend 1⅝ in. (4cm) from the end. String a crystal and bend the wire below it in the opposite

direction of the first bend (**photo d**).

2. Working one end of the wire at a time, make a right-angle bend ¼ in. (6mm) from the crystal (**photo e**).

3. Repeat twice to make a diamond shape with the wire (**photo f**).

4. Fold the excess back against the last bend and trim any extra wire (**photo g**). Repeat on the other side.

5. Slide the diamond-shaped loop onto an end jump ring on the bracelet.

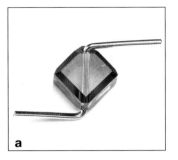

a

b

c

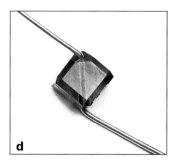

d

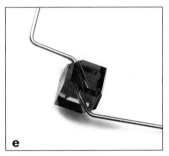

e

f

g

TEMPLATE

Earrings

1. Cut a 3-in (7.6cm) piece of 22-gauge wire.

2. Make a right-angle bend ¼ in. from the end of the wire. Refer to the template and form the earwire's angles as you did the clasp. After you make the diamond shape, roll the wire around a pen or dowel to make the curve in the center.

3. Make three crystal links: two as you did for the bracelet, steps 1–3, and one on a head pin.

4. Connect a crystal link to the earwire. Attach a jump ring to the available loop. Connect another crystal link and jump ring. End with the head pin unit.

5. Make a second earring to match the first.

— *Anna Nehs*

MATERIALS

bracelet 7 in. (18cm)
- **9** 6mm Swarovski crystal cubes with offset holes
- **9** square soldered jump rings
- **10** in. (25cm) 20-gauge wire, half-hard

earrings
- **6** 6mm Swarovski crystal cubes with offset holes
- **4** square soldered jump rings
- **6** in. (15cm) 22-gauge wire, half hard
- **2** 1-in. (2.5cm) 22-gauge head pins

Tools: roundnose pliers, chainnose pliers, flatnose pliers, diagonal wire cutter, ¼ in. (6mm) dowel

Hoop it up

Create your own hoop earrings with sterling wire, pearls, gemstones, and crystals

a

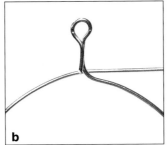

b

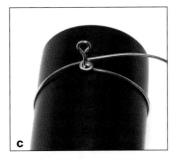

c

d

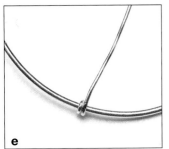

e

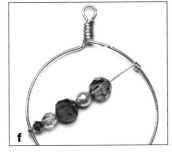

f

g

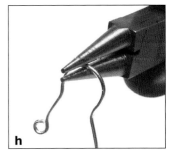

h

i

j

Crystal earrings

1. Cut a 7-in. (18cm) piece of 20-gauge wire. Wrap it snugly around a film canister or small bottle. Bend the wire upward approximately 1½ in. (3.8cm) from one end (**photo a**).

2. With roundnose pliers, make a loop (Basics, p. 8) ¼ in. (6mm) above the circle. Bend the tail down so it is flush with the stem and trim it where it meets the circle (**photo b**). File the end, if necessary.

3. Wrap the remaining tail around the stem from the bend to the loop (**photo c**). Trim the excess wire and remove the hoop from the canister or bottle (**photo d**).

4. Cut a 4-in. (10cm) piece of 24-gauge wire. Wrap one end tightly around the hoop two or more times (**photo e**). Trim the short wire end.

5. String assorted beads on the wire. To connect the wire, wrap it around the hoop as before and trim the excess wire (**photo f**).

6. Repeat steps 4 and 5, attaching wires to the hoop and existing wires as desired (**photo g**).

7. To make an earring wire, cut a 2-in. (5cm) piece of 20-gauge wire. Make a plain loop at one end. Using your fingers or roundnose pliers, bend a curve in the wire ¼ in. above the loop. Bend the wire outward, as shown,

and trim the excess (**photo h**). File the end.

8. Open the loop on the earring wire and attach the loop of the beaded hoop. Close the loop (**photo i**).

9. Make a second earring the mirror image of the first.

Pearl earrings

1. Follow steps 1-3 of the crystal earrings.

2. Cut a 12-in. (30cm) piece of 24-gauge wire. Starting at the top of the hoop near the stem, wrap one end of the wire around the hoop tightly two or more times. Trim the tail wire.

3. String beads as desired and continue to wrap the wire around the hoop (**photo j**).

materials

crystal earrings

- **18–22** 4–8mm assorted crystals, pearls, or glass beads
- 18 in. (46cm) 20-gauge sterling silver wire, half-hard
- 24 in. (46cm) 24-gauge sterling silver wire, dead soft

pearl earrings

- **30** 3–4mm pearls
- 18 in. (46cm) 20-gauge sterling silver wire, half-hard
- 20 in. (46cm) 24-gauge sterling silver wire, dead soft

Tools: chainnose and roundnose pliers, wire cutters, metal file or emery board, film canister or small bottle

When you reach the stem, wrap the wire two or more times and trim the excess.

4. Complete the earrings as in steps 7–9 for the crystal earrings.

— *Naomi Fujimoto*

Cat's eye bracelet

Glowing cat's eye beads
combine with pearls and crystals
for a feminine look

Bracelet

1. This bracelet is 8 in. (20cm) long, including the clasp. Measure your wrist and cut a piece of flexible beading wire 2 in. (5cm) longer than your wrist measurement.

2. String a crimp bead and half of the toggle clasp. Bring the wire through the crimp bead and crimp it (**photo a** and Basics, p. 8).

3. String a 6mm crystal bicone, a pearl, a rhinestone rondelle, a cat's eye bead, and a 6mm round crystal (**photo b**). Repeat this pattern to the desired length.

4. String a bicone and a crimp bead. Go back through the crimp bead, the bicone, the round crystal, and the cat's eye bead, leaving a small loop (**photo c**).

5. Place the loop over the jaw of the roundnose pliers (**photo d**) and tighten the wire by pulling gently on it.

6. Crimp the crimp bead and trim the tail. The end of the bracelet should look like **photo e**.

7. String a 4mm crystal bicone on a head pin (**photo f**).

8. Make a small wrapped loop (Basics) above the bicone (**photo g**).

9. Using two pairs of chainnose pliers, open a jump ring (Basics) and attach the beading wire loop, the wrapped loop, and the other half of the toggle (**photo h**). Close the jump ring (Basics).

Earrings

1. String a crystal bicone, a pearl, a rhinestone rondelle, and a cat's eye bead on a head pin.

2. Make a wrapped loop (Basics) over the cat's eye bead and trim the wire.

3. Using two pairs of chainnose pliers, open the ring at the bottom of an earring finding (Basics) and attach the loop. Close the ring.

4. Make a second earring to match the first.

— *Maryann Humes*

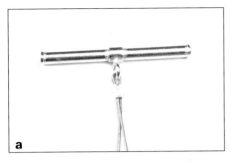

a

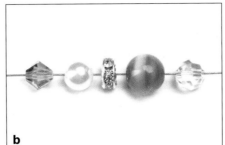

b

c

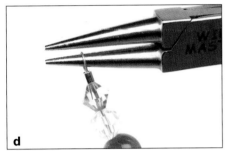

d

e

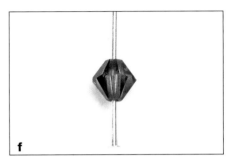

f

g

h

materials

bracelet 8 in. (20cm)

- strand 8mm cat's eye beads, lavender (Fire Mountain Gems 800-355-2137, firemountaingems.com)
- **6** 6mm crystal rhinestone rondelles, silver-plated (Fire Mountain Gems)
- **6** 6mm pearls
- Swarovski crystals
  7 6mm bicones, light amethyst
  7 6mm round, crystal AB
  4mm bicone, amethyst
- 2-in. (5cm) silver head pin
- flexible beading wire, .012–.014
- silver toggle clasp
- 6 x 4mm unsoldered silver oval jump ring (Fire Mountain Gems)
- **2** crimp beads

earrings

- **2** 8mm cat's eye beads, lavender
- **2** 6mm rhinestone rondelles
- **2** 6mm pearls
- **2** 6mm Swarovski crystal bicones, light amethyst
- **2** 3-in. (7.6cm) silver head pins
- pair lever-back earring wires (Fire Mountain Gems)

Tools: roundnose pliers, **2** pair chainnose pliers, diagonal wire cutters, crimping pliers

Attitude adjustment

1. Cut a piece of leather twice the circumference of your wrist. String a pattern of heishe and silver beads for about 3 in. (7.6cm) (**photo a**).

2. Wrap the leather around a cylindrical object, such as a drinking glass or plastic bottle, so the ends overlap. Tape the ends (**photo b**).

3. Cut 2 ft. (61cm) of leather and slide it under the two strands. Make alternating square knots, beginning on the left. For the first half of the knot, cord 1 goes over cords 2 and 3. Cord 4 goes over 1, under 2 and 3, and through the loop made by cord 1 (**figure 1** and **photo c**). To complete the knot, cord 1 goes over 2 and 3. Cord 4 goes over 1, under 2 and 3, and through the loop made by cord 1 (**figure 2** and **photo d**). Continue for about 2½ in. (6cm). Untape the bracelet and remove it from the cylinder.

4. Turn the stitching over and weave the pair of leather ends through two knots (**photo e**). Trim the ends.

5. On each of the remaining ends, string one or two beads. Tie an overhand knot (Basics, p. 8) at the ends to secure the beads (**photo f**).

6. Tie a second overhand knot above the beads. Use an awl or pin to slide the knot so it is snug against the beads (**photo g**). To adjust the fit, pull on the beaded ends.

— *Karin Buckingham*

String a casual bracelet with an adjustable closure
for fun weekend wear

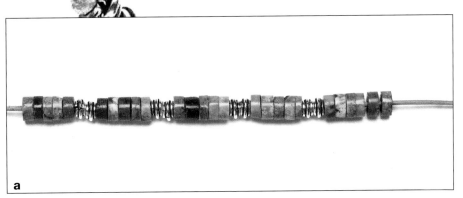

a

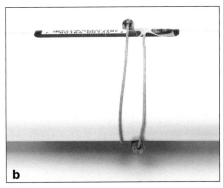

b

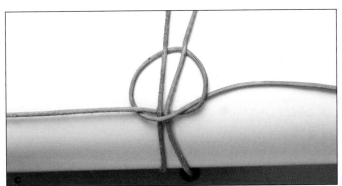

c

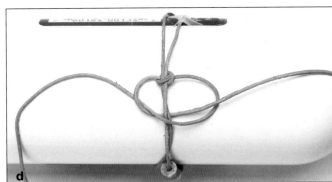

d

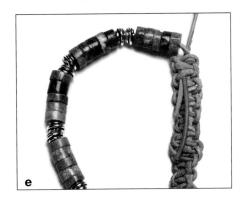

e

f

g

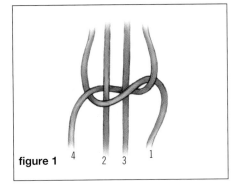

figure 1   4   2   3   1

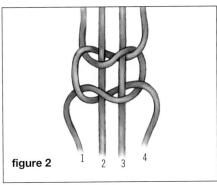

figure 2   1   2   3   4

materials
- 16-in. strand 6mm turquoise heishe beads
- **12** 5mm spacer beads
- 4 ft. 1mm leather cord

Tools: awl or pin, cylindrical form

Fine filigree

Connect filigree findings
and crystals for a bracelet and earring set
with a vintage look

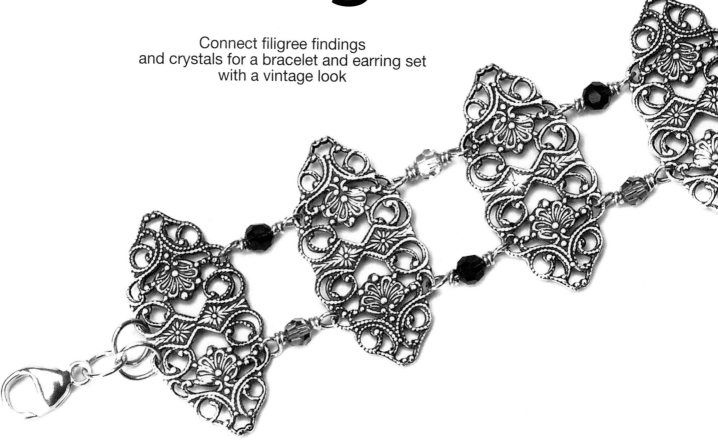

a

b

c

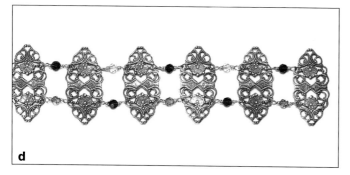

d

e

f

g

h

i

j

Bracelet

1. Make the first half of a wrapped loop (Basics, p. 8) on a 2½-in. (6cm) piece of wire and connect it to the edge of a finding about a third of the way from one end. Complete the wraps and trim the wire tail (**photo a**).

2. String a burgundy crystal onto the wire and make the first half of a wrapped loop next to the bead. Connect the loop to a second finding so that it lines up with the first one. Complete the wraps and trim the excess wire (**photo b**).

3. Repeat step 1 about a third of the way from the other end. String a shadow crystal and connect the findings as in step 2 (**photo c**).

4. Repeat steps 1–3 until you have connected six or more findings. Alternate the crystal colors as shown in **photo d**. Check the fit. Allow 1¼ in. (3cm) for the clasp.

5. Attach two jump rings to the outer edge of one of the findings (Basics). Link another jump ring through these rings, attach a lobster claw clasp to the jump

ring, and close the ring (**photo e**).

6. Repeat step 5 on the other end of the bracelet. Use a soldered jump ring in place of the clasp (**photo f**).

Earrings

1. String a 6mm crystal on a 1½-in. (3.8cm) head pin. Make the first half of a wrapped loop above the bead. Connect the dangle to the bottom loop on a finding (**photo g**). Complete the wraps and trim the excess wire.

2. Cut a 2½-in. piece of wire. Make the first half of a wrapped loop and connect it to the top loop of the finding (**photo h**).

3. String a 4mm crystal and make a wrapped loop above the bead, perpendicular to the previous loop (**photo i**).

4. Open the loop on an earring wire and attach the wrapped loop just made. Close the loop (**photo j**).

5. Make a second earring to match the first.

— Naomi Fujimoto

materials

bracelet 7 in. (18cm)

- **6 or more** filigree findings, approx.16 x 32mm
- **10 or more** 4mm round crystals (5 burgundy, 3 black diamond champagne, 2 shadow crystal)
- 25 in. (64cm) 22-gauge wire, half-hard
- lobster claw clasp and a soldered jump ring
- 6 7mm jump rings

earrings

- 2 filigree findings
- 2 6mm round crystals, burgundy
- 2 4mm round crystals, burgundy
- 5 in. (13cm) 22-gauge wire, half-hard
- 2 1½-in. (3.8cm) head pins
- pair of earring wires

Tools: chainnose and roundnose pliers, diagonal wire cutters

Loops & ladders

Have fun making an easy, two-needle bracelet

Bracelet

1. Cut a 4-ft. (1.2m) piece of Nymo, condition it with beeswax, and thread a needle on each end. String an agate, a spacer, a focal bead, a spacer, and an agate. Center the beads.

2. String three seed beads, a jade bead, and three seeds on both sides of the center row (**photo a**). (A focal bead wider than the 11mm bead shown requires more seeds for the ladder to lie flat. Most 10–11mm centerpieces require five to seven seeds.)

3. String a Czech bead, a jade bead, an agate, a jade, and a Czech on either needle. Continue through the end seed (**photo b**). Set this needle aside. With your second needle, go through the beads on the new row from the opposite direction, picking up the first seed you come to on the other side (**photo c**). Add four to six seeds on each side. (The seed count depends on the width of your row.)

4. Repeat step 3 (**figure 1**), using varied combinations of beads on each row. Continue until you have 15 rows. If you're changing the bracelet's length, continue until you are about two rows shy of half the desired length. The beads for your end rung should be shorter than the other rows.

5. Make a loop of seed beads just big enough to fit around your button. I used 23 seeds for a ⅝-in. (16mm) button (**photo d**). Run both threads through the loop beads and the last rung of your bracelet several times to strengthen this stress point (**figure 2**). Tie the tails together and dab the knot with glue. Pull the ends through the nearest bead then trim the tails.

6. Cut and condition 4 ft. of Nymo, then thread one needle on each end. Center the first row on the thread, and make the second half of the bracelet the mirror image of the first.

7. String eight seed beads on either needle. Slide the button over the beads. Run the needle through the end row to close the loop (**photo e**). Secure the button by running the thread through the loop and end row several times (**figure 3**). Tie the tails together and dab the knot with glue. Pull the ends through the nearest bead then trim the tails.

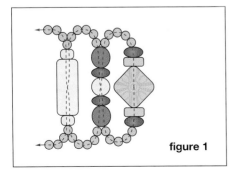

figure 1

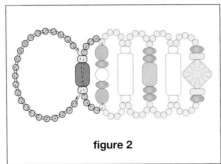

figure 2

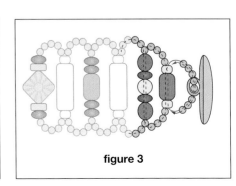

figure 3

a

b

c

d

e

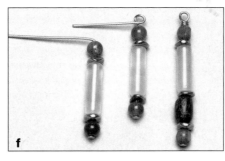

f

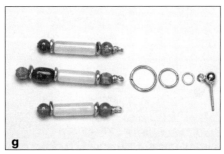

g

materials

bracelet 8-in. (20cm)

- metal focal bead
- **4** metal accent beads
- **14** 14 x 4mm cylindrical gemstone beads, new jade
- **6** 8 x 5mm cylindrical gemstone beads, green turquoise
- **40** 2 x 4mm gemstone beads, jade
- **6** 4mm beads, moss agate
- **12** 4mm Czech pressed-glass 3-sided beads
- **28** seed beads, size 8° matte, gold-lined
- **335** Japanese seed or cylinder beads
- **10** 5mm flat spacers
- Nymo D beading thread
- beeswax
- beading needles, #12
- button with shank, ⅝ in. (16mm) to ⅞ in. (23mm)
- clear glue or nail polish

earrings

- **6** 14 x 4mm cylindrical gemstone beads, new jade
- **2** 8 x 5mm cylindrical gemstone beads, green turquoise
- **4** 4mm Czech pressed-glass 3-sided beads
- **8** 4mm gemstone beads, moss agate
- **14** 5mm flat spacers
- **6** head pins
- **2** 9mm jump rings
- **2** 7mm jump rings
- **2** 4mm jump rings
- pair earring posts

Tools: roundnose and chainnose pliers, wire cutters

Earrings

1. String a Czech bead, a spacer, an 8 x 5mm cylinder, a spacer, a 14 x 4mm cylinder, a spacer, and a Czech bead onto a head pin. Make a wrapped loop (Basics, p. 8). Make two shorter dangles using an agate, a spacer, a 14 x 4mm cylinder, a spacer, and an agate (**photo f**).

2. Connect the earring sections (**photo g**). Open a 9mm jump ring (Basics). Slide on the three dangles with the longest one in the middle. Add a 7mm ring and close the 9mm ring (Basics). Open a 4mm ring, slide on the 7mm ring and one of the posts, and close the rings.

3. Make a second earring to match the first.

— *Melody MacDuffee*

Jump start

Create a
colorful bracelet
with furnace glass
and jump rings
while learning basic
jump ring
construction

materials

bracelets 7½ in. (19cm)

multicolor bracelet

- **17** furnace glass beads
- **16** jump rings, 7–8.5mm inside diameter, 16- or 18-gauge wire
- **17** 5mm coiled rings
- **17** accent beads: size 8º or 6º seed beads, size 5º triangles, or 4mm cubes

black-and-white bracelet

- **23** jump rings, 7–8.5mm inside diameter, 16- or 18-gauge wire
- **23** 4–5mm silver beads with a large hole
- **23-34** accent beads: size 8º or 6º seed beads, size 5º triangles, or 4mm cubes

both projects

- **2** 5mm jump rings
- toggle clasp

Tools: **2** pair chainnose pliers or pair chainnose and pair bent chainnose pliers

Multicolor bracelet

1. Hold a large jump ring with two pairs of pliers, positioning one pair of pliers on each side of the jump ring's opening (**photo a**).

2. Open the jump ring by pulling one side of the ring toward you and pushing the other side away from you, twisting the ends out of plain (**photo b**).

3. String a coiled ring, a furnace glass bead, a coiled ring, and an accent bead on the jump ring (**photo c**).

4. Close the jump ring by reversing steps 1 and 2.

5. Open a second large jump ring. Slide it through one of the coiled rings on the first jump ring (**photo d**).

6. String a furnace glass bead on one side of the open jump ring, so it falls on the opposite side of the furnace glass on the first jump ring. Then string an accent bead on the other side of the jump ring (**photo e**). String a coiled ring and close the jump ring.

7. Open a large jump ring and slide it through the coiled ring strung in the previous step (**photo f**). Repeat step 6.

8. Repeat steps 5–7 until you have one large jump ring remaining.

9. Open a small jump ring and slide it through the loop on one clasp component and an end coiled ring. Close the jump ring (**photo g**). Repeat at the other end of the bracelet with the remaining clasp half.

10. Open the last large jump ring and string an accent bead and a furnace glass bead. Slide the large jump ring onto the small jump ring that connects to the loop on the round half of the clasp. Close the jump ring (**photo h**).

Black-and-white bracelet

1. Open a large jump ring, following steps 1–2 for the multicolor bracelet.

2. String a silver bead, a furnace glass bead, and an accent bead. Close the jump ring.

3. Open a large jump ring and slide it through the previous jump ring (**photo i**).

4. Repeat step 2.

5. Repeat steps 3–4 and connect the remaining large jump rings. Alternate the placement of the furnace glass bead on each jump ring as you did in step 6 for the multicolor bracelet.

6. Use small jump rings to connect the clasp to the end jump rings on the bracelet.

— Catherine Hansen VanderBerg

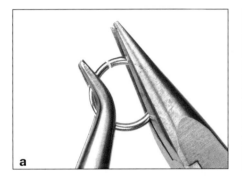

a

b

c

d

e

f

g

h

i

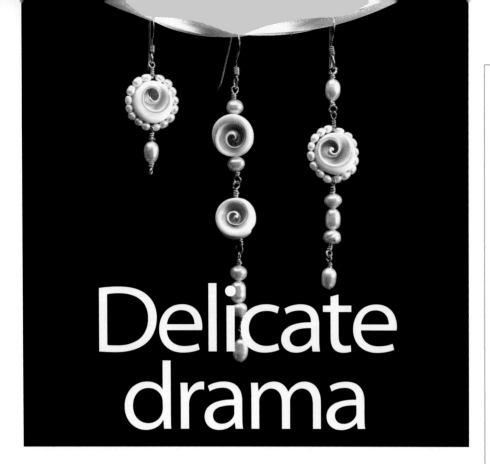

Delicate drama

Shells and pearls combine for a delicate, feminine earring design

materials
short encircled shell earrings
• **2** shell beads (Eclectica, 262-641-0910, eclecticabeads.com)
• **2** 5mm potato pearls
• **32-34** 3mm rice pearls
• **4 in.** (10cm) 24-gauge wire

long dangle earrings
• **4** shell beads
• **4** 6mm rice pearls
• **8** 5mm potato pearls
• **18 in.** (45cm) 24-gauge wire

long encircled shell earrings
• **2** shell beads
• **6** 6mm rice pearls
• **8** 5mm potato pearls
• **32-34** 3mm rice pearls
• **10 in.** (25cm) 24-gauge wire

all projects
• **2** 3-in. (7.6cm) ultra-thin head pins
• **2** French ear wires
Tools: roundnose and chainnose pliers, diagonal wire cutters

Short encircled shells (left)

1. Cut 2 in. (5cm) of wire and make a wrapped loop (Basics, p. 8) at one end. String a 6mm pearl, then make another wrapped loop in the same plane as the first (**photo a**).

2. String a shell bead on a head pin and bend the tail to form a right angle. Bend the tail around the shell and string enough 3mm pearls to encircle half of it. String the pearl component and add enough 3mm pearls to finish encircling the shell (**photo b**).

3. Cross the tail under the starting point and make a wrapped loop. Open the loop on an ear wire (Basics), string the shell component, and close the loop (**photo c**).

4. Make a second earring to match the first.

Long dangles (center)

1. String a 6mm pearl on a head pin and make a wrapped loop (**photo d**).

2. Cut 3 in. (7.6cm) of wire and start a wrapped loop, stringing the pearl component before finishing the wraps. String a 5mm pearl, a 6mm pearl, and a 5mm pearl, then make another wrapped loop (**photo e**).

3. Cut 3 in. of wire and start a wrapped loop, stringing the component from step 2 before finishing the wraps. String a shell, then make another wrapped loop (**photo f**).

4. Cut 3 in. of wire and start a wrapped

loop, stringing the shell's loop from step 3 before finishing. String a 5mm pearl, a shell, and a 5mm pearl. Start another wrapped loop, stringing the ear wire before finishing.

5. Make a second earring to match the first.

Long encircled shells (right)

To combine these two projects, substitute an encircled shell for the two plain shells in the center of the long dangle earrings.

— *Diane Jolie*

Girl's best friend

Imitate the timeless look of the classic diamond tennis bracelet using Japanese seed beads, crystals, and right-angle weave

1. Pick up eight cylinders and slide them 10 in. (25cm) from the end of a 3-yd. (2.7m) length of Fireline. Sew back through the beads again and continue through the next two beads, pulling the beads into a tight circle (**figure 1, a–b**).

2. Pick up an A crystal, skip the next pair of cylinders, and sew through the following pair in the opposite direction so the crystal lies diagonally across the circle (**b–c**).

3. Pick up six cylinders and sew back through the last two beads from the previous step (**c–d**). Reinforce the stitch by repeating the thread path.

4. Repeat step 2 (**d–e**), then sew through the next two cylinders (**e–f**).

5. Repeat step 3 but continue through the next two cylinders (**figure 2, a–b**). This will offset the placement of the next two crystals.

6. Repeat step 2, substituting a B crystal for the A crystal (**b–c**). All the crystals will lie in the same direction.

7. Repeat step 3 (**c–d**). Reinforce the new circle by repeating the thread path and exit at point **d**.

8. Repeat step 6 and sew through the next two cylinders (**d–e**).

9. Repeat steps 5–9, alternating between two color A and two color B crystals.

materials
bracelet 7 in. (18cm)
- 4mm bicone crystals
  26 in color A
  24 in color B
- 3g Japanese cylinder beads
- toggle clasp
- Fireline 6 lb. test or Power Pro 10 lb. test
- beading needles, #12

10. To add the clasp, modify the directions as follows: Add the last crystal, but don't sew through the next two cylinders. Pick up one cylinder and half the clasp and sew back through the cylinder (**figure 3, a–b**). Reinforce the last circle with a second thread path, making sure to sew back through the clasp at least one more time. Secure the tail with half-hitch knots (Basics, p. 8) between a few beads and trim.

11. Repeat on the other end of the bracelet.

— *Anna Nehs*

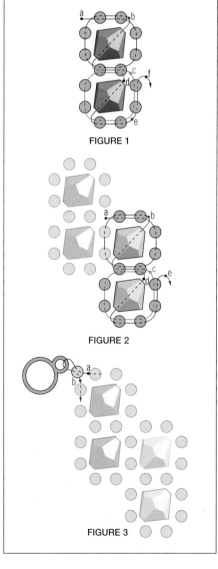

FIGURE 1

FIGURE 2

FIGURE 3

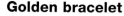
Create a sophisticated look with two-strand links and gemstones

Simply strung

Silver bracelet

1. On a 24 in. (61cm) length of beading wire, string a silver bead, a crimp bead, a silver bead, and one end of a toggle clasp. Slide the clasp and the beads to the center. Go back through the beads and the crimp with the wire. Tighten it to form a small loop around the clasp. Crimp the crimp bead (Basics, p. 8).

2. Slide a bead cap and pearl onto the doubled wire. String a silver bead and a spacer on each wire (**photo a**).

3. On each wire, string an amethyst bead, a spacer, a pearl, and a spacer. Slide a calla link onto both wires.

On each wire, string a spacer, a pearl, and a spacer (**photo b**).

4. Repeat step 3 three times.

5. On each wire, string an amethyst, a spacer, and a silver bead. Thread both wires through a pearl, a cap, a silver bead, a crimp, a silver bead, and the other clasp part. Snug up the beads, then go back through the silver beads and the crimp bead.

6. Tighten this wire to form a small loop around the clasp. Crimp the crimp bead. Cut the excess wire tails.

Golden bracelet

1. Open a jump ring using two pliers (Basics). Slide the toggle ring and the single loop on the end bar onto the jump ring. Close the ring.

2. Cut two 12 in. (30cm) lengths of beading wire. Pass one wire through an end bar loop. String a crimp bead and a spacer on the wire and the tail. Repeat with the second wire. String a calla link on both wires. Pull the wires so the tails measure 1 to 2 in./2.5-5cm (**photo c**).

3. Crimp the crimp bead.

4. String a spacer, a sunstone bead, and a spacer on each long wire, then add a glass bead. String a spacer, a sunstone, and a spacer on each wire, then add a link (**photo d**).

5. Repeat step 4 three times.

6. String a spacer and a crimp bead on one wire. Pass the wire through a loop on the other end bar and back through the crimp bead, the spacer, and the link. Repeat with the other wire.

7. Tighten all the beads, then pull both wires to create small loops around the end bar loops. Crimp the crimp bead. Trim the four wire tails against the two links.

8. Open a jump ring. Slide the toggle bar and the single loop of the end bar onto this ring. Close the ring. Open another ring. Slide the end ring and the charm on this ring. Close the ring (**photo e**).

Earrings

1. String a silver bead, a bead cap, an amethyst bead (**photo f**), another cap, and two more silver beads onto the head pin.

2. Cut the pin with wire cutters, leaving ⅜ in. (1cm) above the bead. Make a loop (**photo g** and Basics). Pass an earring finding through the loop.

3. Make the other earring.

— *Pam Arion and Julie Young*

a

b

c

d

e

f

g

EDITOR'S NOTE: To determine the bracelet length that's right for you, measure your wrist and add 1 to 1½ in. (2.5-3.8cm). Changing a length is easy, but it requires planning ahead. You can add or remove a few beads at the ends or add or remove a link.

materials

silver bracelet 8 in. (20cm)
- **4** calla links, pewter with antique-silver finish
- **10** 6 x 9mm amethyst barrel beads
- **18** 6mm pearls
- **8** 3mm sterling silver beads
- **2** 7mm fairy skirt bead caps
- **36** 4mm heishi spacers or 3mm daisy spacers
- **2** crimp beads
- toggle clasp
- **24** in. (61cm) flexible beading wire, .014–.015

golden bracelet 7½ in. (19cm)
- **5** calla links, pewter in antique-gold finish
- **4** 14 x 10mm 2-hole vintage green glass beads
- **16** 6 x 4mm sunstone beads
- **2** end bars, 2-to-1 loops, pewter in antique-gold finish
- **36** 4mm heishi spacers or 3mm daisy spacers
- **4** crimp beads
- **4** 5mm jump rings
- toggle clasp
- Art Nouveau flower charm, pewter in antique-gold finish
- **24** in. (61cm) flexible beading wire, .014–.015

earrings
- **2** leftover amethyst beads
- **4** fairy skirt bead caps
- **6** 3mm silver beads
- **2** ball-end head pins
- **2** earring findings

Tools: wire cutters, roundnose and chainnose pliers, crimping pliers

Mermaid mesh

Link a three-layer chain mail bracelet

Although this mesh is not difficult to create, it requires correct proportions between the ring diameter and the wire gauge to make the pattern flow. If you vary from the materials listed here, you'll need to experiment to find other sizes and gauges that will allow this mesh to work up easily and move freely. Before you begin, antique the 4mm jump rings in a solution of liver of sulfur (following the manufacturer's directions). Darkening the smaller rings gives the pattern its distinctive 3-D look. The directions tell you how many and which color jump rings to open in each step. Remember to close each jump ring after linking it to a neighboring ring or rings.

Main bracelet section

1. Open four large silver rings (Basics, p. 8) and connect them to three small black rings (**photo a**).
2. Close three large silver rings and open four large silver rings. Place one closed silver ring over the left black ring. Place the second closed silver ring over the middle black ring (**photo b**). Secure them in position with an open silver ring through the left and middle blackened rings (**photo c**). Make sure the silver ring grabs only the two black rings. This new ring sits on top of the second layer of silver rings.
3. Place the third closed ring over the

right black ring and lock it in place with an open silver ring. This silver ring grabs the middle and right black rings (**photo d**, p. 88).
4. Attach one open silver ring to the far left black ring and one to the far right black ring (**photo e**).
5. Open four black rings. Starting on the left, take one black ring and grab the silver ring sandwiched beneath the top and bottom row of silver rings (**photo f**).
6. Use the second black ring to grab the two silver rings sandwiched beneath the top and bottom row of silver rings (**photo g**). Use the third black ring to grab the next pair of silver rings. Connect the fourth ring on the far right as you did the first in step 5. Place these black rings above or in front of the previous row of black rings.
7. Open three silver rings. Place one silver ring through the first and second black rings added in steps 5 and 6 (**photo h**). Place the next silver ring through the second and third black rings and the third silver ring through the third and fourth black rings.
8. Open three black rings. Connect them to silver rings as in steps 5 and 6, but this time each black ring grabs two rings from the silver layer below (**photo i**). Make sure the black rings are above or in front of the previous row of black rings.
9. Open four silver rings. Place one

silver ring through the left black ring. Place the second silver ring through the left and middle black rings. Place the third silver ring through the middle and right black rings. Place the fourth silver ring around the right black ring (**photo j**).
10. Open four black rings. Repeat steps 5 and 6. This completes the pattern.
11. Repeat steps 7–10 until you reach the desired length for the main bracelet section. Allow about 1½ in. (38mm) for tapering the bracelet and adding the clasp.

d

e

f

g

h

i

j

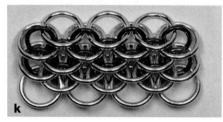

k

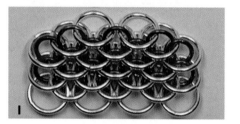

l

m

n

Tapered ends and clasp

1. To taper one end, open three silver rings. Attach the rings as in step 7, **(photo k)**.

2. Open three black rings. Attach the black rings to the three silver rings as in step 8.

3. Open two silver rings. Attach one between the first and second black rings and the other between the center and end black ring as in step 9 **(photo l)**.

4. Open two black rings. Attach each one to two silver rings in the layer below as in step 8.

5. Attach one silver ring to the two black rings **(photo m)**.

6. Attach one clasp half to the end ring **(photo n)**.

7. Repeat steps 1–6 on the other end of the bracelet.

— *Anne Mitchell*

materials
bracelet 7 in. (18cm)

- 2 troy oz. (62.2grams) sterling silver jump rings, 6.5mm inside diameter, 18-gauge wire (annemitchell.net code: SS)
- 1 troy oz. (31.1 grams) sterling silver jump rings, 4mm inside diameter, 19-gauge wire (code: KK)
- toggle clasp
- liver of sulfur
- padded work surface

Tools: 2 pair chainnose pliers or 1 pair chainnose and 1 pair bent chainnose pliers

EDITOR'S NOTE: Troy weight is an ancient system of measuring precious metals and gemstones. One troy oz. equals 31.10 grams.

Sparkle plenty

Turn a lively mix of crystals into a dazzling bracelet

a

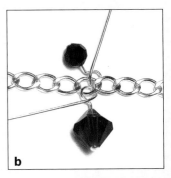

b

c

materials

bracelet 7½–8 in. (19-20cm)

- 1 ft. (30cm) dapped curb link 5.2mm chain
- **16–20** 10mm bicone crystals
- **18–22** 8mm round crystals
- **18–22** 6mm bicone crystals
- **22–28** 6mm round crystals
- **16–20** 4mm cube crystals
- **90–94** 2-in. (5cm) head pins
- **2** 6mm split rings
- toggle clasp

Tools: chainnose and roundnose pliers, wire cutters

1. Determine the finished length of your bracelet and cut a piece of chain to that length.

2. String each crystal on a head pin and make the first half of a wrapped loop (Basics, p. 8, and **photo a**).

3. Slide the bead units onto the chain (**photo b**) and complete the wraps. Continue building the bracelet, staggering sizes and colors of crystals. Work on both sides of the chain and attach several units per link for maximum fullness.

4. Attach a split ring to the end link of chain. Attach a clasp half to the split ring (**photo c**). Repeat on the other end of the bracelet with the other clasp half.

— *Karin Buckingham*

Button bracelet

Gemstone chips and buttons combine for an easy, three-strand bracelet

1. Cut three pieces of flexible beading wire 9 in. (22.8cm) long. On one end of each wire string a crimp bead, a 3mm bead, and one loop on one half of the clasp. Go back through the 3mm and the crimp bead, tighten the wires, and crimp the crimp beads (Basics, p. 8, and **photo a**).

2. String approximately 1½ in. (3.8cm) of gemstone chips on each of the wires.

3. Slide on a spacer bar. Check to see that all three strands are about even. You can see from the picture (**photo b**) that there is a gap before the spacer bar in the first strand. Adjust your strands accordingly by adding, removing, or just rearranging mismatched gemstone chips.

4. Slide a button on the center strand. Place a chip of about the same width as the button shank on each of the outside wires and slide on another spacer bar (**photo c**).

5. String about 1 in. (2.5cm) of gemstones after the spacer.

6. Repeat steps 3–5 until all the buttons have been strung. String 1½ in. (3.8cm) of gemstone chips after the last spacer.

7. Hold up the bracelet vertically to see that all of the elements are lined up evenly.

8. String a crimp bead, a 3mm bead,

and one loop from the other clasp half on each of the wires. Make sure the two halves of the clasp are set in the correct position (**photo d**). Tighten the wires and crimp the crimp beads.

— *Anne Nikolai Kloss*

EDITOR'S NOTE: Select buttons that do not have a long shank. Buttons with long shanks will sit higher than your beaded strands and may wobble.

materials
bracelet 7½ in. (19cm)
- 5 shank buttons
- 2 3-hole spacer bars for each button
- 2 16-in. strands of gemstone chips
- 6 crimp beads
- 6 3mm silver accent beads
- 3-loop slide clasp, silver
- 27 in. (69cm) .012–.014 flexible beading wire

Tools: crimping or chainnose pliers

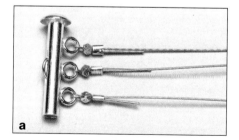

Make a pair of long, lean earrings in just a few minutes

Long on style

1. Determine the desired length of each earring's beaded section. Add 3 in. (76mm), and cut two pieces of flexible beading wire to that length.

2. String a seed bead, a crimp, a seed, an accent bead, if desired, and a briolette or drop bead. Turn and go back through these beads. Tighten the wire and crimp the crimp bead (Basics, p. 8 and **photo a**). Trim the short tail close to the end seed bead.

3. String an assortment of beads on the wire. End with a seed bead (**photo b**).

4. String a crimp bead and a seed bead. Go back through the last beads strung and tighten the wire, leaving a small loop. Crimp the crimp bead and trim the excess wire (**photo c**).

5. Attach the loop to an earring finding (**photo d**).

6. Make a second earring to match or complement the first.

— *Naomi Fujimoto*

a

b

c

d

materials
one pair of earrings
- **2** briolettes or other drop beads
- pairs of assorted gemstones and crystals
- assorted small beads and spacers
- 1g seed beads, size 11º
- flexible beading wire, .012–.014
- **2** earring findings
- **4** crimp beads

Tools: chainnose or crimping pliers, diagonal wire cutters

Jewelry Sets Chapter 3

Forever amber

Amber nuggets and a pendant create a timeless necklace and earrings set

a

b

c

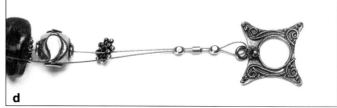

d

e

f

Necklace

1. Determine the finished length of your necklace. (This one is 18 in./46cm.) Add 6 in. (15cm) and cut a piece of beading wire to that length. Center the pendant and string a round spacer and 1½ in. (3.8cm) of nuggets on each side (**photo a**).
2. Tape one end. On the other end, string a flat spacer, 20mm bead, flat spacer, two nuggets, flat spacer, 20mm bead, and flat spacer (**photo b**).
3. String 1½ in. of nuggets and a flat spacer. Repeat this pattern three more times. End with another flat spacer (**photo c**).
4. String a 10mm bead, flat spacer, round spacer, crimp bead, round spacer, and half the clasp. Go back through the last three beads (**photo d**). Tighten the

wire but do not crimp the crimp bead.
5. Remove the tape and repeat steps 2–4 on the other side of the pendant. Check the fit and add or remove beads, if necessary. Crimp the crimp beads (Basics, p. 8) and trim the excess wire.

Earrings

1. String a head pin with a flat spacer, nugget, flat spacer, and 8mm round bead. Make a wrapped loop (Basics and **photo e**) above the top bead.
2. Slightly open the earring wire hook, attach the bead unit, and close the hook (**photo f**). Make a second earring to match the first.

— *Rupa Balachandar*

materials

necklace 18 in. (45.7cm)
- amber pendant
- 16-in. (41cm) strand of amber nuggets, 8-12mm
- 4 20mm silver oval or cylinder beads
- 2 10mm silver round or oval beads
- 18 8mm flat spacers
- 6 3mm round spacers
- 2 crimp beads
- flexible beading wire, .014 or .015

earrings
- 2 amber nuggets (remaining from necklace)
- 2 8mm round silver beads
- 4 5mm flat spacers
- 2 2-in. (5cm) head pins
- pair of hook earring wires

Tools: chainnose and roundnose pliers, crimping pliers (optional), wire cutters

Combine gemstone beads and silver components for a complex-looking set

Floating slider set

Necklace

1. Cut three 21-in. (.53m) pieces of beading wire.

2. String 1¾ in. (4.5cm) of 3mm garnets to the center of two wires and 3½ in. (9cm) on the third. Position the slider over the beads (**photo a**).

3. String a silver spacer, a garnet rondelle, and another spacer on each of the three wires (**photo b**).

4. String groups of 7–20 garnets separated by a spacer, a rondelle, and a spacer on each strand. Make sure these accents don't line up vertically, which can happen due to size differences in the beads. Arrange the strands so the one with 3½ in. of garnets is in the middle.

5. Check the fit, allowing 1½ in. (3.8cm)

for finishing the ends. Adjust the length by adding or removing an equal number of garnets on both ends of each strand.

Finishing

1. Cut a 3-in. (7.6cm) piece of wire.

2. Make a 1/16 in. (2mm) or smaller wrapped loop (Basics, p. 8) at one end of the wire.

3. Remove the tape from the top-right strand. String a crimp and the wrapped loop. Go back through the crimp bead and several of the garnets (**photo c**). Tighten the wire and crimp the crimp bead (Basics).

4. Repeat step 3 with the remaining strands on the right side of the necklace.

5. String a cone and a 4mm garnet on

the wire. Start a wrapped loop above the garnet (**photo d**). Slide a lobster claw clasp in the loop and finish the wraps.

6. Repeat steps 1–5 on the other end of the necklace, attaching 1½ in. (3.8cm) of chain in place of the clasp.

7. Slide a 4mm garnet and a spacer on a head pin. Start a wrapped loop and slide it into the last link of the chain. Finish the wrap (**photo e**).

a

b

c

d

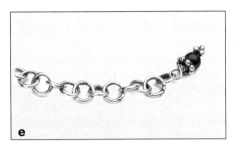

e

f

g

Bracelet

Make the bracelet with the following changes to the necklace instructions:
1. Cut three 10-in. (25cm) pieces of beading wire.
2. Repeat steps 2–3, stringing 2 in. (5cm) of garnets on the middle strand.
3. Repeat step 4, stringing groups of 3–10 garnets that are separated by spacers and rondelles.
4. Check the fit on your wrist, adding or removing beads as necessary.
5. Finish the bracelet the same way as the necklace.

Earrings

1. Thread a garnet on a head pin and make a wrapped loop. Repeat twice.
2. Cut a 3-in. wire. Start a wrapped loop an inch (2.5cm) from one end. Slide on the three dangles. Finish the wrap (**photo f**).
3. String a spacer and a silver bead. Make a wrapped loop (**photo g**).
4. Slide the dangle on the ear wire.
5. Repeat steps 1–4 to make the other earring.

— *Nina Cooper*

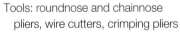

materials

necklace 19 in. (48.2cm)
- **30** 5mm garnet rondelles
- **3** 4mm round garnet beads
- **3** 16-in. (41cm) strands 3mm round garnet beads
- **65** 4mm silver daisy spacers
- **1⁷⁄₁₆ in. (3.7cm) curved slider
- **2** small cones
- **63** in. (1.3m) flexible beading wire, .012 or .014
- **6** in. (15cm) 24-gauge wire, half-hard
- **1½** in. (3.8cm) chain
- **6** small crimp beads
- lobster claw clasp
- decorative head pin, 24-gauge

bracelet 7½ in. (19cm)
- **2** 16-in. (41cm) strands 3mm round garnet beads
- **16** 5mm garnet rondelles
- **3** 4mm round garnet beads
- **32** 4mm silver daisy spacers
- **1⁷⁄₁₆** in. (3.7cm) curved slider
- **2** small cones
- **1½** in. (3.8cm) chain
- **30** in. (.76m) flexible beading wire, .012 or .014
- **6** in. (15cm) 24-gauge wire, half-hard
- **6** small crimp beads
- lobster claw clasp
- decorative head pin, 24-gauge

earrings
- **6** 3mm round garnet beads
- **2** 4mm silver daisy spacers
- **2** 6mm silver beads
- **6** decorative head pins, 24-gauge
- **6** in. (15cm) 24-gauge wire, half-hard
- **2** hook earring findings with garnet

Tools: roundnose and chainnose pliers, wire cutters, crimping pliers

Hip to be square

String lustrous, cube-shaped beads to create a contemporary lariat with matching earrings

Necklace

1. Alternate three cube beads with four seed beads on a head pin (**photo a**). Trim the head pin to ⅜ in. (1cm) above the top bead and turn a plain loop (Basics, p. 8).

2. String two head pins with two triangle beads, two with three triangle beads, and two with four triangle beads (**photo b**). Trim each head pin to ⅜ in. above the top bead and turn a plain loop on each.

3. Slide all seven head pins on a split ring, as if adding keys to a key ring, to complete the dangle (**photo c**).

4. Cut a 33-in. (.84m) length of beading wire. String 2 in. (5cm) of triangle beads and slide them to one end of the wire. String a crimp bead on the long end, against the beads (**photo d**).

5. Loop the wire's short end through the last triangle bead and the crimp bead (**photo e**). Tighten the wire and crimp the crimp bead (Basics). Trim the excess wire.

6. Alternating seed beads and cubes, string seven color A cubes and one color B cube (**photo f**). Then string six color A cubes and two color B cubes. Continue reducing the number of A cubes and increasing the number of B cubes until you've strung a run of seven B cubes.

7. String a seed bead, a crimp bead, a seed bead, and the dangle completed in step 3 onto the wire. Go back through the last few beads (**photo g**). Tighten the wire and crimp the crimp bead. Trim the excess wire.

Earrings

1. Alternating seed beads and cube beads, string an A cube and a B cube on a head pin. Turn a plain loop above the top bead. Repeat steps 2 and 3 of the necklace (**photo h**).

2. Attach the split ring to the earring wire (**photo i**). Make a second earring to match the first.

3. For a smaller pair of earrings, omit the head pin with cube beads (**photo j**).

— *Linda Augsburg*

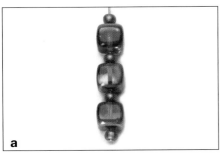

a

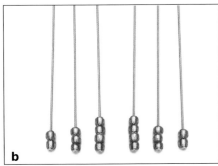

b

c

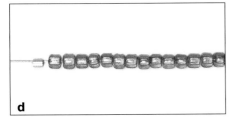

d

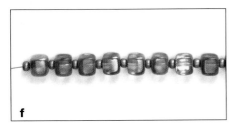

f

h

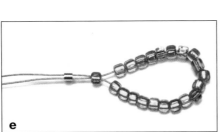

e

g

i

j

materials

necklace 27 in. (.68m)
- 2 16-in. (41cm) strands 7mm cube-shaped glass beads, 1 each of 2 colors
- 70 seed beads, size 6º
- 80 Czech triangle beads, size 10º or 11º
- 7 2-in. (5cm) head pins
- flexible beading wire, .014 or .015
- 6mm split ring
- 2 crimp beads

earrings
- leftover beads from necklace
- 14 2-in. (5cm) head pins
- 2 6mm split rings
- 2 earring wires

Tools: chainnose and roundnose pliers, wire cutters, split ring pliers (optional), crimping pliers (optional)

99

Summer set

A glass shell bead, crystals, and simulated opals make a magical combination

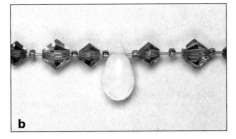

Necklace

1. Cut a 20-in. (50cm) length of flexible beading wire and slide the shell to the center. This necklace is 18 in. (46cm) long without the clasp. The organic shape requires some balancing with seed beads around the holes so it hangs properly. This one has an 11º and a 6mm simulated opal on each side (**photo a**).

2. String a small spacer, a green bicone, a large spacer, a 10mm amethyst, a small spacer, and a green bicone. This pattern will not repeat.

3. String a small spacer, an 8mm opal, and a small spacer. This is group one.

4. Group two is strung as follows: green bicone, green 15º, purple bicone, green 15º, opal briolette, green 15º, purple bicone, green 15º, green bicone (**photo b**).

5. Alternate groups one and two until you've strung seven 8mm opals and six briolettes.

6. String a small spacer, a 6mm opal, a small spacer, and a green bicone.

7. String an 11º, a crimp bead, and an 11º.

8. Go through one end of the clasp and back through the two seeds and the crimp bead. Pull the tail tight and crimp the crimp bead (Basics, p. 8 and **photo c**).

9. Repeat steps 2–8 to finish the other side. Trim the tails.

Earrings

1. Cut a 4-in. (10cm) length of 24-gauge half-hard sterling silver wire.

2. Start a wrapped loop (Basics) and add a briolette (**photo d**). Finish the wraps (**photo e**).

3. String a purple bicone, a small spacer, a green bicone, a large spacer, a 10mm amethyst, a large spacer, a green bicone, a small spacer, and a purple bicone (**photo f**). Make a small wrapped loop above the purple bicone.

4. Open the bottom loop of the earring finding (Basics), attach the briolette component, and close the loop (Basics).

5. Make a second earring to match the first.

— *Debbie Nishihara*

materials

necklace 18 in. (46cm)

- shell bead (Eclectica, 262-641-0965, eclecticabeads.com)
- simulated opal beads:
  12 10mm briolettes
  2 8mm rondelles
  4 6mm rondelles
- **2** 10mm faceted amethyst rondelles
- crystal bicones:
  30 5mm, light olivine
  24 4mm, tanzanite
- seed beads:
  6 size 11º, purple
  50 size 15º, green
- **4** 11mm silver spacers
- **30** 4mm silver spacers
- flexible beading wire, size .014
- **2** crimp beads
- toggle clasp (Green Girl Studios, 828-298-2263, greengirlstudios.com)

earrings

- **2** 10mm opal briolettes
- **2** 10mm amethysts
- **4** 5mm bicones, light olivine
- **4** 4mm bicones, tanzanite
- **4** 11mm silver spacers
- **4** 4mm silver spacers
- **8** in. (20cm) 24-gauge sterling silver wire (Rio Grande, 800-545-6566)
- **2** earring wires

Tools: roundnose and chainnose pliers, wire cutters, crimping pliers

Here's the scoop

Round and curved links of chain create a ruffled,
feminine look for a necklace and earring duo

a

b

c

d

e

f

g

h

materials

necklace 15½ in. (39cm)

- **20-25** 4mm bicone crystals (**7** each of fuchsia and smoky quartz, **4** lavender, **3** light sapphire)
- **20-25** 4-5mm faceted gemstone rondelles (**7** iolite, **7** pink tourmaline, **4** aquamarine, **3** citrine)
- 18 in. (46cm) bar-and-link chain
- **40-50** 1½-in. (3.8cm) head pins
- lobster claw clasp
- **2** 18-gauge jump rings or **2** split rings

earrings

- **8** 4mm bicone crystals (**2** each of fuchsia, smoky quartz, lavender, and light sapphire)
- **6** 4-5mm faceted gemstone rondelles (**2** each of iolite, pink tourmaline, and citrine)
- **14** 1½-in. head pins
- **2** earring wires

Tools: chainnose and roundnose pliers, diagonal wire cutters, split-ring pliers (optional)

Necklace

1. To make a drop, string each bead on a head pin and make the first half of a wrapped loop (Basics, p. 8 and **photo a**).

2. Leave the first round link of chain open. At the next available round link, attach a drop (**photo b**).

3. Complete the wraps (**photo c**).

4. Alternate the patterns shown in **photo d** three times, until the chain is ¾ in. (2cm) shorter than the desired length. (This necklace is 15½ in./39cm.) The necklace may end in the middle of a pattern.

5. Leave the next round link open and cut off the next curved link. Attach a jump ring (Basics) or a split ring to each round end link. Attach a lobster claw clasp to the ring (**photo e**).

Earrings

1. Cut two segments of chain, each with four round links and three curved links.

2. String each bead on a head pin and make the first half of a wrapped loop. Attach a crystal head pin to the bottom link (**photo f**). Complete the wraps.

3. Attach drops to the chain as shown and complete the wraps (**photo g**). Leave the top link open.

4. Repeat with the remaining chain segment and drops.

5. Open an earring wire loop and attach it to the top link of one chain. Close the loop. Attach the remaining earring wire to the other top link of chain.

— *Naomi Fujimoto*

Midas touch

Amethyst beads and brass spacers give regal elegance to a necklace, bracelet, and earring set

a

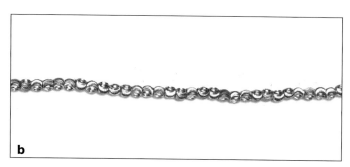

b

c

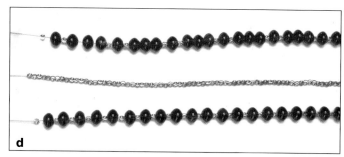

d

e

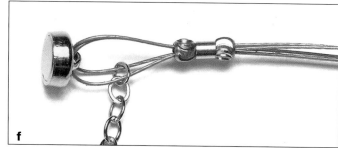

f

Necklace

1. Determine the finished length of your necklace based on the shortest strand. (This one is 16 in./41cm.) Add 6 in. (15cm) and cut a piece of beading wire to that length. Cut a second piece 1 in. (2.5cm) longer than the first, and a third 1 in. longer than the second. On the shortest (inner) strand, string a six-bead pattern as shown in **photo a**. Repeat this pattern to 1 in. of your desired length. Tape the ends.

2. On the middle strand, string a length of brass beads an inch longer than the inner strand (**photo b**). Tape the ends.

3. On the longest (outer) strand, string an alternating pattern of amethyst and brass beads an inch longer than the middle strand (**photo c**). Tape the ends.

4. Arrange the strands so the shortest strand is at the top and the longest is at the bottom (**photo d**).

5. On one end of each strand, string a brass bead, a crimp bead, a brass bead, and half the clasp. Go back through the last beads strung on each strand (**photo e**). Tighten the wires, check the fit, and add or remove beads as needed. Crimp the crimp beads (Basics, p. 8) and trim the tails. Repeat on the other end using the clasp's soldered jump ring.

Bracelet

1. Determine the desired length of your bracelet, add 5 in. (13cm), and cut two pieces of beading wire to that length. Over both strands, string a brass bead, a crimp bead, a brass bead, half the clasp, and the end link of chain. (The chain adds security to a bracelet with a magnetic clasp.) Go back through the beads (**photo f**). Tighten the wires, but do not crimp the crimp bead.

2. String an amethyst over both working strands. Separate the strands and string three brass beads, an amethyst, and three brass beads on each wire (**photo g**, p. 106). Repeat this pattern until you are an inch short of the desired length. End with an amethyst over both strands.

3. Finish the bracelet as in step 1, using

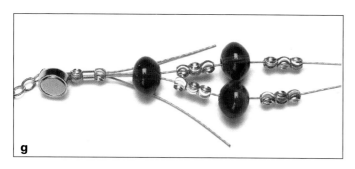

g

h

i

j

the other clasp half and the other end link of the chain. Check the fit. Add or remove beads on each end and shorten the chain, if necessary. Tighten the wire and crimp the crimp beads. Trim the excess wire (**photo h**).

Earrings

1. String an alternating pattern of amethyst and brass beads on a hoop finding (**photo i**).

2. Using chainnose pliers, slightly bend each end of the hoop upward (**photo j**). Make a second earring to match the first.

— *Paulette Biedenbender*

materials

necklace 18 in. (46cm)

- **2** 16-in. (41cm) strands 5mm button-shaped amethyst beads
- **3** 16-in. strands 2mm round brass beads, wave cut (Beads Forever, 510-526-1800, beadsforever.com)
- flexible beading wire, .014 or .015
- hook clasp with soldered jump ring
- **6** crimp beads

bracelet 7½ in. (19cm)

- **22** button-shaped amethyst beads
- **88** brass beads
- flexible beading wire, .014 or .015

- 3 in. (7.6cm) 2mm flat cable chain
- magnetic clasp
- **2** crimp beads

earrings

- **4** brass beads
- **6** amethyst beads
- **2** gold-filled hoop findings

Tools: chainnose or crimping pliers, diagonal wire cutters

It's a
wrap

Combine assorted gemstones with chain for an adjustable-length necklace and dangling earrings

a

b

c

d

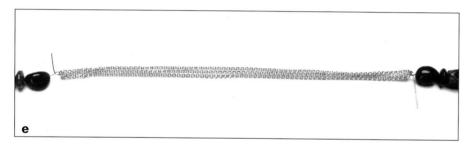

e

materials

necklace 53 in. (1.35m)

- 16-in. (41cm) strand 15–19mm gemstone rondelles
- 16-in. strand 15 x 23mm gemstone nuggets
- 16-in. strand 10 x 14mm faceted gemstones
- 16-in. strand 4-6mm gemstone buttons
- 9 ft. (2.7m) or more 2.8mm cable chain
- 4 ft. (1.2m) 22-gauge silver wire

dangle earrings

- 2 faceted gemstones
- 8 gemstone buttons
- 2 1½-in. (3.8cm) head pins
- 2 earring wires

chain earrings

- 8 gemstone buttons
- 5 in. (13cm) 2.8mm cable chain
- 4 1½-in. head pins
- 2 earring wires

Tools: chainnose and roundnose pliers, diagonal wire cutters

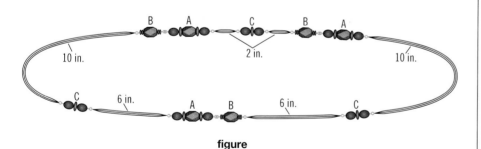

B A C B A

10 in.   2 in.   10 in.

C   6 in.   A B   6 in.   C

figure

Necklace

1. Cut six 5-in. (13cm) and three 3-in. (7.6cm) lengths of wire. Make the first half of a wrapped loop (Basics, p. 8) at one end of each wire.

2. Refer to the figure and string three pattern As and three Cs on the 5-in. wires. On the 3-in. wires, string pattern B (**photo a**).

3. Make the first half of a wrapped loop perpendicular to the bottom loop (**photo b**).

4. Attach an A and a B unit by linking the loops and completing the wraps

(**photo c**). Repeat with the other A and B units.

5. Cut six 10-in. (25cm), six 6-in. (15cm), and six 2-in. (5cm) lengths of chain. Refer to the figure as you work the following steps.

6. Attach three 6-in. lengths of chain to one loop of an A/B unit. Complete the wraps (**photo d**). Attach three 6-in. lengths of chain to the unit's other loop and complete the wraps.

7. Attach one loop of a C unit to the three chains at one end. Attach another C unit to the chains at the other end

(**photo e**). Complete the wraps.

8. Attach three 10-in. lengths of chain to the open loop of either linked C unit, and the other end of the chain segments to one loop of an A/B unit. Complete the wraps. Repeat on the other end.

9. On each end, attach three 2-in. lengths of chain to each open A/B unit. Complete the wraps. Attach the open ends of the chain segments to a C unit. Complete the wraps.

To wear the necklace, wrap it around your neck twice and adjust the length as desired.

f

g

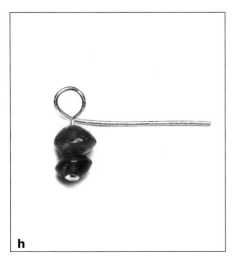

h

i

j

Dangle earrings

1. String two gemstone buttons, one faceted gemstone, and two buttons on a head pin (**photo f**). Make a wrapped loop above the beads.

2. Open an earring wire and attach the dangle (**photo g**). Close the earring wire. Make a second earring to match the first.

Chain earrings

1. Cut one 1-in. (2.5cm) and one 1½ in. (3.8cm) lengths of chain.

2. String two buttons onto a head pin and make the first half of a wrapped loop (**photo h**). Make a second beaded head pin.

3. Slide each head pin into the end link of one length of chain and complete the wraps (**photo i**).

4. Open an earring wire and slide the chains onto the wire (**photo j**). Close the earring wire.

5. Make a second earring the mirror image of the first.

— *Karin Buckingham*

Earth colors and
textured silver accent a
gemstone necklace
and bracelet set

Tawny
asymmetrics

a

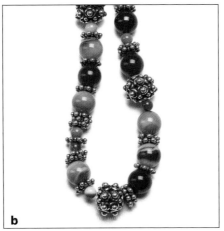

b

c

d

materials

necklace 18 in. (46cm)
- 40-50 4–10mm round gemstones
- 8 8–10mm silver beads, assorted styles
- 60 4–6mm spacers, assorted styles
- 2 crimp beads
- toggle clasp or S-hook
- 2 soldered jump rings
- flexible beading wire, .014 or .015

bracelet 7½ in. (19cm)
- 15 4-10mm round gemstones
- 3 8-10mm silver beads, assorted patterns
- 20 4-6mm spacers, assorted styles
- 2 crimp beads
- flexible beading wire, .014 or .015
- toggle clasp

Tools: chainnose or crimping pliers, diagonal wire cutters

Necklace

1. Determine the finished length of your necklace. (This one is 18 in./46cm.) Add 6 in. (15cm) and cut a piece of beading wire to that length. Center the largest bead on the wire (**photo a**).

2. In the spirit of planned asymmetry, begin building your necklace on each side of the focal bead, staggering the placement of the largest beads so they fall in different places on each end (**photo b**). Continue until the necklace is 1 in. (2.5cm) shorter than the desired length.

3. On each end, string a spacer, a crimp bead, a spacer, and half the clasp. Go back through these beads and a few more (**photo c**). Tighten the wires, check the fit, and add or remove beads, if necessary. Crimp the crimp beads (Basics, p. 8) and trim the excess wire.

Bracelet

1. Determine the finished length of your bracelet, add 5 in. (13cm), and cut a piece of beading wire to that length. String a random pattern of gemstones, silver beads, and silver spacers until the bracelet is 1 in. shorter than the desired length.

2. On each end, string a crimp bead, a spacer, and half the clasp. Go back through these beads and a few more (**photo d**).

3. Tighten the wires, check the fit, and add or remove beads, if necessary. Crimp the crimp beads (Basics) and trim the excess wire.

— *Beth Wheeler*

Inside story

Open-center beads
encase crystals in a geometric
necklace and bracelet

**EDITOR'S NOTE: Use crimping pliers to make rounded crimps — the spacers
will easily cover them.**

a

b

materials

aqua necklace 16 in. (41cm)
- **5** open-center geometric beads, diamond-shaped (Eclectica, 262-641-0910, eclecticabeads.com)
- **5** 6mm bicone crystals
- **12** 4mm bicone crystals
- **6** 4-5mm large-hole spacers
- **1** ft. (30cm) silver chain
- **2** crimp beads
- lobster claw clasp with **2** split rings
- flexible beading wire, .014 or .015

aqua or burgundy bracelet 7½–8 in. (19–20.3cm)
- **6** or **7** open-center beads, diamond-shaped or circular
- **6** or **7** 6mm bicone crystals, bicones for diamond-shaped beads or round for circular beads
- **14-16** 4mm crystals, bicone or round
- **7** or **8** 4-5mm large-hole spacers
- **4** 3mm round silver beads
- **2** crimp beads
- toggle clasp
- flexible beading wire, .014 or .015

Tools: crimping pliers, diagonal wire cutters

c

d

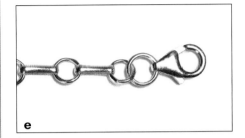

e

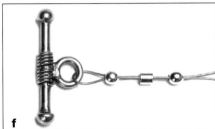

f

g

h

Necklace

1. Cut the chain in half, making two 6-in. (15cm) segments with an equal number of links.

2. Cut a 9-in. (23cm) piece of beading wire. (This necklace is 16 in./41cm. For a longer necklace, cut 1 ft./30cm of beading wire.) String a crimp bead, a 4mm crystal, and the end link of a chain segment. Go back through the beads (**photo a**). Tighten the wire and crimp the crimp bead (Basics, p. 8).

3. String a large-hole spacer and a 4mm crystal over the wire tail. Slide the spacer over the crimp. Trim the excess wire (**photo b**).

4. String an open-center bead with a 6mm crystal inside, 4mm crystal, spacer, and 4mm crystal (**photo c**). Repeat this pattern three times (or more for a longer necklace), then string an open-center bead with a 6mm crystal inside.

5. String a 4mm crystal, crimp bead, spacer, 4mm crystal, and the end link of the remaining chain segment. Go back through these beads (**photo d**). Tighten the wire and crimp the crimp bead. Trim the excess wire. The spacer will slide over the crimp.

6. Check the fit, allowing about ½ in. (1.3cm) for the clasp. For a shorter necklace, cut equal lengths of chain from each end. On one end, attach a split ring and a lobster claw clasp to the end link of the chain (**photo e**). To finish the other side, attach a split ring to the end link of chain.

Bracelet

1. Determine the finished length of your bracelet, add 5 in. (13cm), and cut a piece of beading wire to that length. String a 3mm round bead, crimp bead, round bead, and half the clasp. Go back through the beads (**photo f**) and tighten the wire. Do not crimp the crimp bead yet.

2. String a 4mm crystal, spacer, 4mm crystal, and open-center bead with a 6mm crystal inside. Repeat this pattern until the bracelet fits comfortably around your wrist. End with a 4mm crystal (**photo g**).

3. String a 3mm round bead, crimp bead, round bead, and the remaining clasp half. Go back through the last few beads (**photo h**). Tighten the wire and check the fit. Add or remove an equal number of beads from each side, if necessary. Crimp the crimp beads (Basics) and trim the excess wire.

— *Gloria Farver*

Fabulous facets

Combine pearls and crystals for a luxurious necklace and earrings set

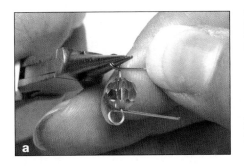

Necklace

1. Determine the length of your necklace. The first three strands in this necklace are 16½ in. (42cm), the next three are 17 in. (43cm), and the bottom three are 17½ in. (44.5cm).

2. Cut approximately 155 pieces of chain, ranging in length from ¼ in. (6.4mm) to ¾ in. (1.9cm). Cut approximately 155 2¼ in. (5.7cm) lengths of wire.

3. Use a jewelry design board to determine the bead placement in your strands. Lay out three strands at a time by placing an assortment of beads randomly spaced in the grooves of the design board. Spaces between beads will be filled with wrapped loops that connect the varied lengths of chain. Remember to allow about ½ in. (1.3cm) for the wrapped loops on each bead.

4. Center a bead on a length of wire and begin a wrapped loop (Basics, p. 8) on each end (**photo a**). Repeat for the rest of the beads in the strands.

5. Start assembling each strand at the center. Attach the end link of a piece of chain to a loop on the center bead and complete the wrap. Attach a piece of chain to the other side of the bead the same way. Attach a loop on the next bead to the other end of the chain and complete that wrap (**photo b**).

6. Continue adding beads and chain to each side of the strand until you have reached the desired length. Build the second and third strands the same way as the first, checking the placement of the beads as you go and making adjustments as necessary.

7. Follow steps 3–6 to complete the second and third groups of strands.

8. Attach a split ring to each loop on the clasp.

9. Attach the first group of three strands to the top split ring on each half of the clasp. You can attach some strands by connecting the wrapped loop on the last bead to the split ring and attach others by threading the end link of chain onto the split ring (**photo c**). Repeat to connect the second and third groups of strands to the corresponding split rings.

Earrings

1. Cut a 2-in. (5cm) length of wire and string a square crystal to the center. Begin a wrapped loop on both ends.

2. Cut a piece of chain three links in length and connect them to the top loop. Complete that wrap.

3. String a pearl on one head pin and a round crystal on another and begin a small wrapped loop above each bead. Cut two pieces of chain, one 13 links long, and the other six links long. Thread the 13-link chain on the pearl's loop and the six-link chain on the crystal's loop. Complete the wraps.

4. Thread the other end of each chain onto the loop below the square crystal and complete the wrap.

5. If needed, stretch the top link above the crystal with a tapestry needle and thread it onto the loop on the earring finding. Close the loop. Make the second earring the mirror image of the first.

— Alice Korach

materials

neoklaco 18 in. (46cm)

- **2** strands 10mm oblong pearls
- **16-in.** (41cm) strand 7.5mm round faceted pearls
- **48** 6mm round Swarovski crystals
- **18** 6mm square Swarovski crystals
- **30–36 ft.** (9–11m) 24-gauge gold-filled wire
- **7–8 ft.** (2–2.5m) 2.2mm gold-filled cable chain
- **6** 4.5–5mm gold-filled split rings
- **3-strand** gold clasp

earrings

- **2** 6mm square crystals
- **2** 6mm round crystals
- **2** 7.5mm faceted pearls
- **4** head pins
- **2** earring finding
- **4 in.** (10cm) 24-gauge gold-filled wire
- **5 in.** (13cm) 2.2mm gold-filled cable chain

Tools: roundnose and chainnose pliers, diagonal wire cutters, jewelry design board (optional)

Pearl Clusters

Stitch an ensemble of delicate beaded beads

Necklace

The last bead cluster serves as a button that fits snugly through the beaded loop at the other end, forming a clasp.

1. Using 4 ft. (1.2m) of conditioned Nymo (Basics, p. 8), string 28 size 15º seed beads. Sew through the beads again, forming a loop.

2. String three gold 11ºs (**figure 1, a–b**), a crystal 11º, a pearl, and a crystal 11º (**figure 1, b-c**). Slide the beads against the beaded loop.

3. Sew through the three gold 11ºs again (**figure 2, a–b**), then string a crystal 11º, a pearl, and a crystal 11º (**b-c**).

4. Repeat step 3 four more times, then sew through the three gold 11ºs again (**photo a**, p. 118).

5. String six 15ºs (**photo b**).

6. Repeat steps 3–5 27 times (**photo c**), stopping at step 5 in the last repetition.

7. To strengthen the beading, sew back through the center core of the necklace, up to and around the loop made in step 1.

8. Tie a half-hitch knot (Basics) between beads, then dot the knot with glue. Let dry. Sew through the next few beads, then trim the excess thread.

9. Clasp the necklace by sliding the loop over the last beaded bead.

Drop earrings

1. Using 2 ft. (61cm) of conditioned Nymo, string eight 15ºs. Sew through the beads again, forming a loop.

2. Pick up one 15º. Skip this bead, then sew through the loop and the new 15º.

3. String five 15ºs (**photo d**).

4. Repeat steps 2–6 from the necklace directions five times, stopping at step 5 in the last repetition.

5. Reinforce the work as before, then knot, glue, and trim the thread.

6. Using pliers, open the loop (Basics) on the ear wire, then string the beaded loop (**photo e**). Close the loop.

7. Make a second earring to match the first.

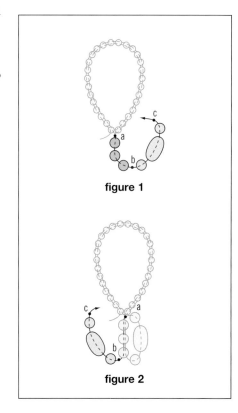

figure 1

figure 2

materials

necklace 15 in. (38cm)
- seed beads
  3g Charlottes size 15º, metallic gold or silver
  2g Japanese size 11º, metallic gold or silver
  2g size 11º, silver-lined crystal

earrings – either pair
- seed beads
  1g Charlottes size 15º, metallic gold or silver
  1g Japanese size 11º, metallic gold or silver
  1g size 11º, silver-lined crystal
- 2 ear wires

all projects
- 2 16-in. (41cm) strands 3 x 4mm rice pearls (140 pearls for necklace and 25 pearls for either earring pair)
- Nymo D, white, conditioned with beeswax or Thread Heaven
- beading needles, #12
- G-S Hypo Cement or nail polish
Tools: chainnose pliers

a

b

c

d

e

Loop earrings

1. Work steps 1–4 from the drop earring directions.

2. Sew through the 15ºs just below the beaded loop, then go through the loop. Pull tight.

3. Knot, glue, and trim the thread.

4. Attach an ear wire as before.

5. Make a second earring to match the first.

— *Melody MacDuffee*

EDITOR'S NOTE: Be sure to use Japanese seed beads where noted in the materials list, so the holes are large enough to allow for multiple thread passes.

Casual clusters

Knot a necklace with multiple layers of beads

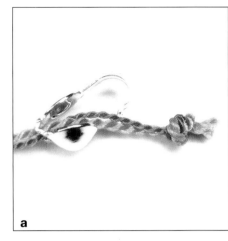

a

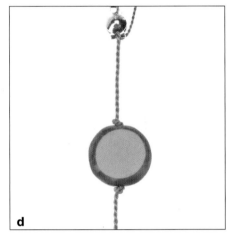

d

This design clusters beads together, so it's a fun way to mix pearls, stones, and glass beads of different shapes and sizes. Use the materials list as a guide for bead counts, but feel free to stray from the sizes and types of beads listed.

1. Unwrap the #8 and #2 cords from their cards, leaving the twisted wire needle on both cords. Tie the tail ends of the #8 and #2 cords together with an overhand knot (Basics, p. 8). Trim the ends of the cords just past the knot.
2. String a clamshell bead tip over both cords with the hook end toward the knot (**photo a**).
3. Dot the knot with glue and close the bead tip over the knot with chainnose pliers (**photo b**).
4. Attach the loop on a clasp half to the hook on the bead tip. Pinch the hook closed with chainnose pliers and pin the clasp end of the cords to the macramé board.
5. Wrap the #2 cord on a card and set it aside.
6. Make a loose overhand knot with the

#8 cord and use a pin or awl to slide the knot to ½ in. (1.3cm) from the bead tip (**photo c**).
7. String a 4mm glass bead against the knot. Make an overhand knot and slide it against the bead just strung (**photo d**). Make another overhand knot ½ in. away from the previous knot.
8. Repeat step 7 until you reach the desired length of the necklace or bracelet minus the length of the clasp.
9. Unwrap the #2 cord from the card and string a color A Charlotte, a rice pearl, a rondelle, a rice pearl, and a color A Charlotte. Position the beads against the bead tip and tie an overhand knot around the #8 cord before the next knot. Use an awl or a pin to position the knot so it is tight and the beads are snug against each other (**photo e**).
10. String a color B Charlotte, 3mm glass bead, silver spacer, 3mm bead, and color B Charlotte. Slide the beads against the knot and tie an overhand knot around the #8 cord past the first 4mm bead (**photo f**).
11. Continue the pattern by repeating

steps 9–10. As you work, keep the knots on the #8 cord and not over other knots.
12. After tying the knot past the last bead, turn the piece and work back toward the clasp, knotting as you did before but with the following pattern: String a color A Charlotte, 3mm bead, silver spacer, 3mm bead, and color A Charlotte. Make an overhand knot around the #8 cord, then string two color B Charlottes, 4mm round stone bead, and two color B Charlottes.
13. Turn the piece and work back toward the other end as follows: String a 6mm pearl, tie an overhand knot around the #8 cord, and string a color C Charlotte, rice pearl, silver spacer, rice pearl, and color C Charlotte.
14. String a bead tip over both cords after the last knot. Make an overhand knot with both cords and use a pin or awl to slide it inside the bead tip.
15. Trim the excess cording, secure the knot with glue, and close the bead tip. Attach the remaining clasp half.

— *Kim Otterbein*

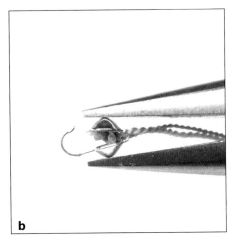

b

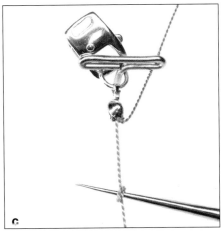

c

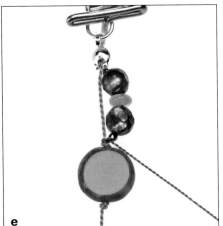

e

f

materials

necklace 17 in. (43cm)

- pearls
  - **90** rice pearls, color A
  - **45** rice pearls, color B
  - **25** 5mm (any shape)
  - **25** 4mm (any shape)
- Czech glass beads
  - **50** 4mm
  - **25** 3mm
- round stone or glass beads
  - **25** 4mm
  - **25** 2mm
- **25** 4mm rondelle-shaped beads
- gold or silver beads
  - **25** 3mm
  - **25** 2mm
- 5g Charlottes size 13º, each of 3 colors, A, B, and C
- **2** clamshell bead tips
- clasp
- Griffin bead cord, #8 and #2
- clear nail polish or G-S Hypo cement

bracelet 8 in. (20cm)

- pearls
  - **36** rice pearls, color A
  - **18** rice pearls, color B
  - **9** 5mm (any shape)
  - **9** 4mm (any shape)
- Czech glass beads
  - **20** 4mm
  - **10** 3mm
- round beads
  - **9** 4mm
  - **9** 2mm
- **9** 4mm rondelle-shaped beads
- gold or silver beads
  - **9** 3mm
  - **9** 2mm
- 3g Charlottes size 13º, each of 3 colors, A, B, and C
- **2** clamshell bead tips
- clasp
- Griffin bead cord, #8 and #2
- clear nail polish or G-S Hypo cement

Tools: awl (optional), T-pins or quilting pins, chainnose pliers, macramé board

Metal works

Casual style takes no time at all with colorful metal shapes

Necklace

1. Cut a 3-in. (7.6cm) length of wire. Make the first half of a wrapped loop (Basics, p. 8) 2 in. (5cm) from the end. String a leaf, a triangle, and a rectangle on the loop (**photo a**). Make two to three wraps just above the metal shapes and trim the excess wire.

2. Make a wrapped loop above the metal shapes with the remaining wire end. Keep this loop parallel to the first and perpendicular to the metal pieces (**photo b**). The wraps should fill the space between the loops.

3. Center the pendant on the leather. (**photo c**)

4. At one end of the leather cord, make a loop large enough to fit over the metal triangle. Tie an overhand knot (Basics)

to secure the loop in place (**photo d**).

5. String a metal triangle on the other end on the leather cord (it will be snug). Check the fit and trim the leather, if necessary. Tie an overhand knot at the cord's end (**photo e**).

6. Tighten the knot and trim the excess cord (**photo f**).

Earrings

Open the loop on the earring wire. Slide a leaf, a triangle, and a rectangle on the loop (**photo g**). Close the loop. Repeat to make a second earring.

— *Linda Augsburg*

materials

- 4 17 x 17mm triangular metal shapes, red
- 3 18 x 22mm rectangular metal shapes, denim blue
- 3 7 x 21mm feather-shaped metal shapes, olive brown (metal shapes available from Fire Mountain Gems, 800-355-2137, firemountaingems.com)
- 3 in. (8cm) 22-gauge wire
- 2 ft. (61cm) 1mm round leather cord
- 2 niobium earring wires

Tools: roundnose and chainnose pliers, diagonal wire cutters

EDITOR'S NOTE: To protect the finish on the wire and earring findings from getting marred by your pliers, fold a small piece of cloth over them while you work.

a

b

c

d

e

f

g

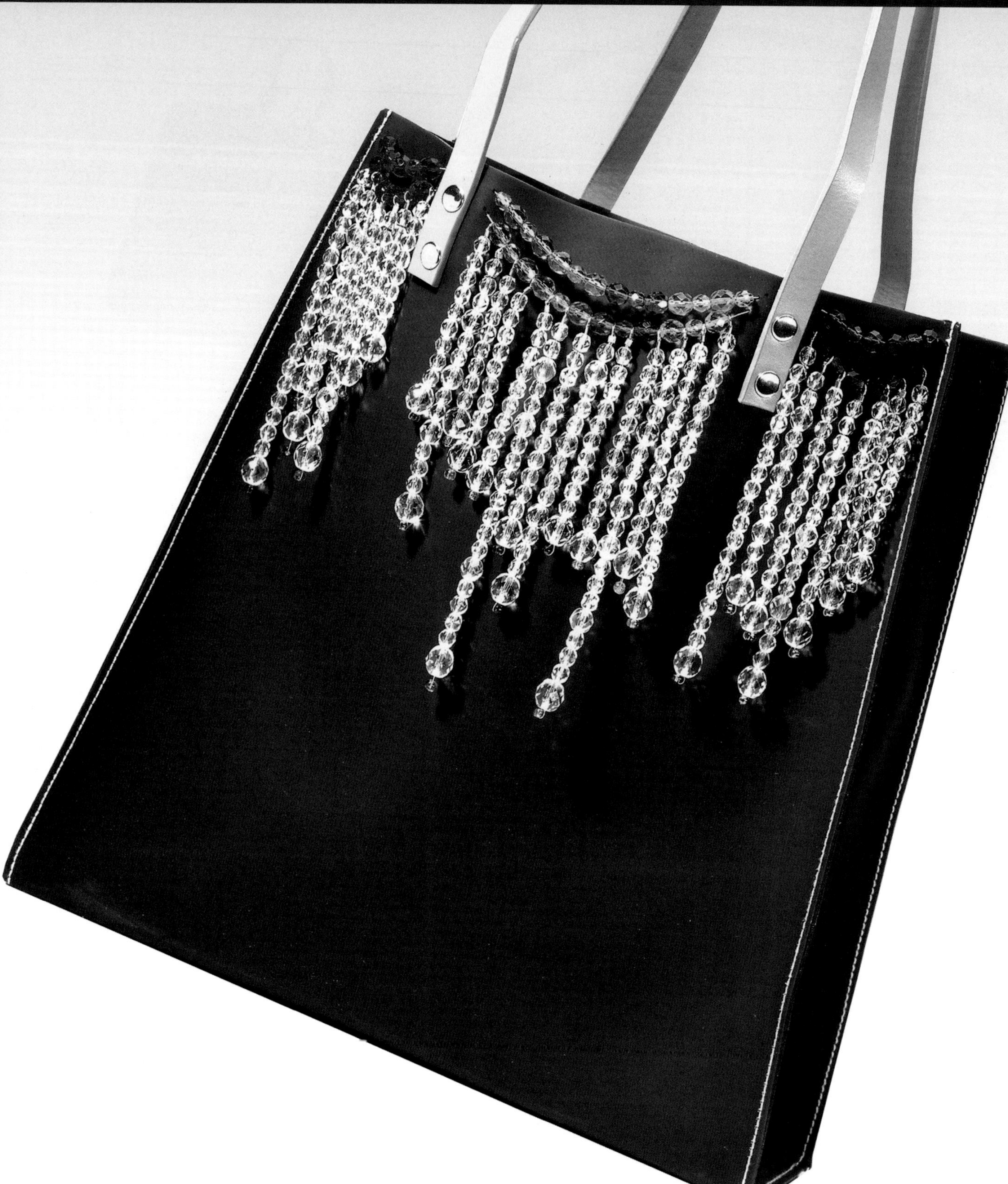

Other Chapter 4
accessories

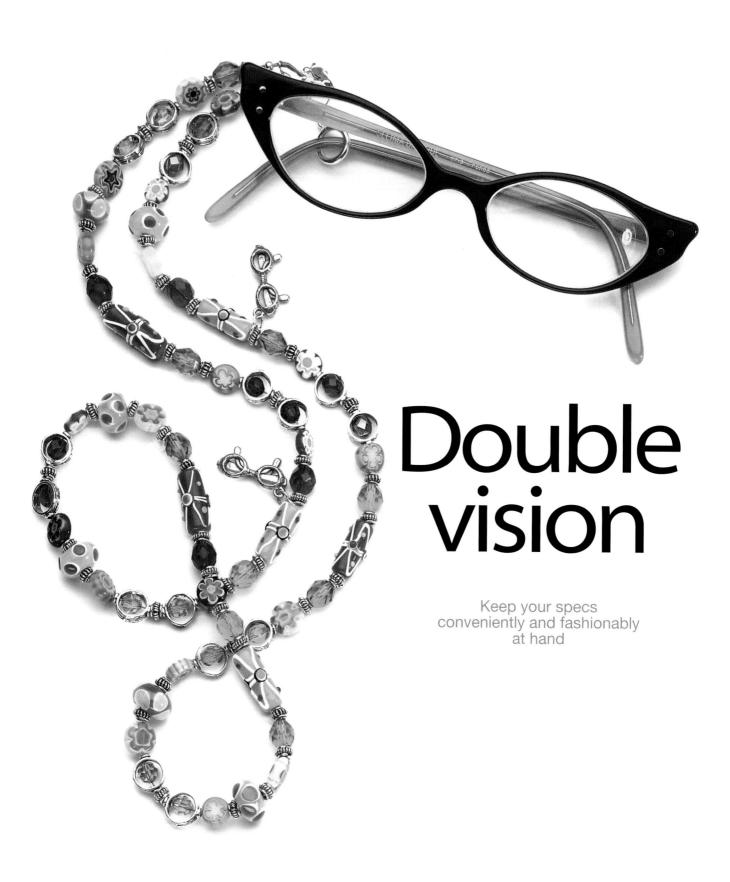

Double vision

Keep your specs conveniently and fashionably at hand

a

b

c

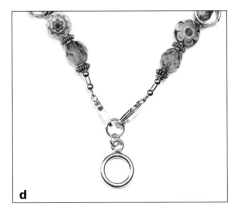

d

e

materials

eyeglass holder 32 in. (81cm)

- **18-26** 10mm millefiori disc-shaped beads
- **4-8** 12mm lampwork beads
- **4-8** 9 x 20mm cylinder beads
- **12-16** 11 x 9.5mm round frame beads (Rio Grande, 800-545-6566, riogrande.com)
- **12-16** 9mm fire-polished Czech crystals
- **12-16** 6mm fire-polished Czech crystals
- **50-60** 4mm flat silver spacers
- **2** charms
- flexible beading wire, .018
- 6mm soldered jump ring
- 5mm jump ring
- 2 4mm jump rings
- 4 2mm round silver spacers
- 2 crimp beads
- loop half of toggle clasp
- 2 lobster claw clasps

Tools: chainnose and roundnose pliers or 2 pairs of chainnose pliers, wire cutters, crimping pliers

1. Open the 5mm jump ring (Basics, p. 8) and connect the small loop of the clasp half and the 6mm jump ring (**photo a**). Close the jump ring.

2. Open a 4mm jump ring and attach a charm. Close the jump ring. Repeat with the other charm.

3. Determine the finished length of your eyeglass holder/necklace. (This one is 32 in./81cm). Add 6 in. (15cm) and cut a piece of beading wire to that length.

4. Tape one end of the wire. String beads and spacers as desired, stringing charms approximately 4 in. (10cm) and 24 in. (61cm) from the beginning (**photo b**). Continue stringing beads and spacers until the strand is within 2 in. (5cm) of the desired length.

5. Remove the tape. On each end, string a round spacer, a crimp bead, a round spacer, and a lobster claw clasp. Go back through the beads just strung plus a few more (**photo c**). Tighten the wire, check the fit, and add or remove beads if necessary. Crimp the crimp beads (Basics) and trim the excess wire.

6. To wear as an eyeglass holder, attach both lobster claw clasps to the 6mm soldered jump ring (**photo d**) and string the temple of your glasses through the large loop of the clasp.

7. To wear as a wrapped necklace, cross and wrap each end around to the back of your neck. Attach both lobster clasps to the soldered jump ring (**photo e**).

— *Jane Konkel*

EDITOR'S NOTE: Arrange beads before stringing, positioning complementary beads adjacent to each other.

Carry on

Beaded accents add a designer's touch
to a discount-store bag

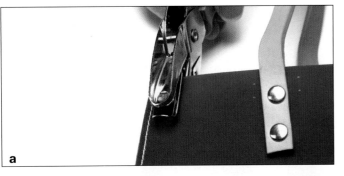

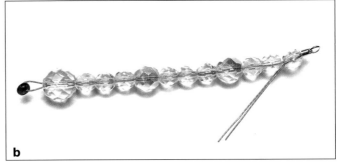

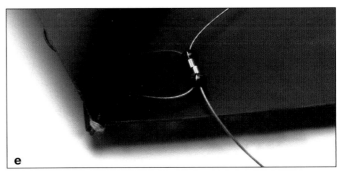

1. Mark one row of dots ¼ in. (6mm) from the top edge and a second row ¼ in. below it as follows: one pair at the edge of the bag, a pair on either side of the handles, and a pair at the opposite edge. Use a micro-hole punch to punch holes in the bag (**photo a**). Repeat on the other side of the bag.

2. Cut four pieces of beading wire 8 in. (20cm) longer than the width of the bag. Set the bag and the wires aside.

3. To make a dangle, cut a piece of beading wire twice your desired length. (These range from 3–5 in./7.6–13cm.) Center a seed bead on the wire. Over both wires, string a 10mm crystal bead, a mix of 6mm and 8mm crystal beads, a crimp bead, and a jump ring. Go back through the crimp bead and crystal (**photo b**). Tighten the wire, crimp the crimp bead (Basics, p. 8), and trim the excess wire.

4. Make enough dangles to span the width of the bag. Match the seed bead colors with your planned trim bead colors.

5. Bring one piece of beading wire from the inside of the bag through to the front, using the top left hole. Begin stringing a pattern of 6mm and 8mm beads. Go back through the next hole (**photo c**). Go behind the handle on the inside of the bag and come out through the next hole. Continue stringing 6mm

and 8mm beads, going around the handles as described. Bring the wire back to the inside of the bag at the other end. Secure the ends with tape.

6. Using the bottom row of holes, string beads as in step 5, but alternate between the beads with dangles. Alternate lengths of dangles and match seed beads colors to trim colors (**photo d**).

7. On the inside of the bag, untape the ends and string a seed bead and a crimp bead over each wire end. Cross the bottom wire through the crimp bead and the seed bead on the top wire and cross the top wire through the crimp bead and the seed bead on the bottom wire (**photo e**). Pull the wires tight and crimp the crimp beads. Repeat on the other end of the bag.

8. Repeat steps 5–7 on the other side of the bag.

— *Karin Buckingham*

materials

- plastic tote bag, 10 x 12 in. (25 x 30cm)
- **60–80** 10mm fire-polished beads, crystal color
- **100–120** 8mm fire-polished beads, crystal color
- **64–84** 8mm fire-polished beads, assorted colors
- **400–420** 6mm fire-polished beads, crystal color
- **64–84** 6mm fire-polished beads, assorted colors
- **68–88** seed beads, size 6º, assorted colors
- **68–88** crimp beads
- **60–80** 4mm soldered jump rings
- flexible beading wire, .019

Tools: chainnose or crimping pliers, wire cutters, micro-hole punch

Accent on brooches

At once retro and totally up-to-date, ribbon brooches are easy to make and a pleasure to wear. Enjoy the splash of color on a lapel or sweater, or try one as an accent on a fabric purse.

Before you start, consider the options: You can make this brooch with or without a leaf and with or without fringe. If you plan to include the leaf, stop after step 5 of the flower instructions, make and attach the leaf as explained on p. 131, then continue at step 6. When you've finished the ribbon components, add the fringe, if desired, as the finishing touch.

Flower

1. Place the pin back against the filigree stamping slightly above center on the front or convex side. Weave a 6-in. (15cm) piece of craft wire through the pin back and stamping to hold them together securely (**photo a**). Hide the wire ends under the filigree.

2. Remove the wire from one edge of the ribbon. Using a yard (.9m) of thread, make tiny stitches close to that edge from end to end (**photo b**). Pull the thread ends to gather the ribbon tightly, and knot them together. Stitch the raw edges together (**photo c**).

3. Use the ribbon wire to gather the other edge. Pull gently on both ends of the wire at the same time, gathering the ribbon until the edge is about the same diameter as the filigree (**photo d**). Twist the wires together and trim them to ¼ in. (6mm). Hide the wire under the ribbon.

4. Distribute the ruffles evenly around the flower. Shape the flower so the outer edge is slightly raised.

5. Place the flower on the filigree with the pin back facing out and toward the top. Sew beads to the center of the flower (**photo e**) to hide the ribbon's center opening, and at the same time, sew through the flower to attach the filigree. (If you plan to add a leaf to your brooch, skip to the leaf instructions. Then come back to step 6, below.)

6. When you're done adding beads, bring the needle out through the back of the flower. Stitch the edge of the flower to the edge of the filigree, working all the way around (**photo f**). Secure the thread in the ribbon and trim.

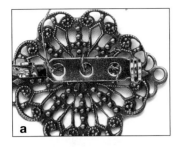

a

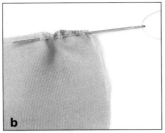

b

c

d

e

f

g

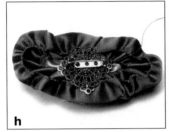

h

i

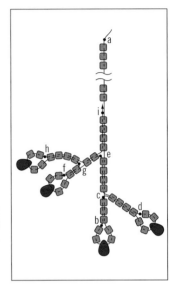

Leaf (optional)

1. Gather the green ribbon into a circle by pulling on both wires along one edge. Twist the wires together to secure them. Repeat with the wires along the other edge, but don't make as tight a circle (**photo g**).

2. Pinch the circle's smaller opening closed, shaping the ribbon into an oval.

3. Sandwich the leaf between the flower and the filigree. Make sure the leaf's smaller opening is behind the flower and facing front. Center the flower and filigree, so you have an equal amount of the leaf showing on each side (**photo h**).

4. Starting at one end of the leaf and working with the back facing you, stitch the ribbon's edges together to close the opening. As you approach the filigree, fold the leaf's upper and lower edges so you can tuck them under it. Stitch through both the leaf and the flower as you sew them to the filigree (**photo i**). Continue sewing around the filigree. Close the opening between the ribbon's edges on the other side of the flower, as before.

5. Pinch the ribbon's oval shape slightly to resemble leaves. Hide the cut edges in the folds and gathers.

Fringe (optional)

This design calls for three strands of branched fringe. Each branch consists of a pair of short fringes. Space the fringes evenly across the bottom of the filigree.

1. Before starting the fringe, secure 2 yd. (1.8m) of thread in the ribbon behind the lower edge of the filigree. Come out through the filigree and pick up 30 seed beads for the stem, a teardrop, and two seed beads (**figure, a–b**). Skip the last two beads, the teardrop, and two beads and continue through three beads on the stem (**b–c**).

2. Pick up six beads, a teardrop, and two beads (**c–d**). Skip two beads, the drop, and two beads. Continue through the first four beads added in this step and the next four beads along the stem (**d–e**).

3. To make the remaining pairs of short fringes, pick up six beads, a drop, and two beads (**e–f**). Skip two beads, the drop, and two beads, and continue through two beads (**f–g**). Pick up six beads, a drop, and two beads (**g–h**). Continue through the first four beads on this branch and four on the stem (**h–i**).

materials
one brooch
- 14 in. (36cm) 1½-in.-wide (3.8cm) French wired ribbon, flower color
- 14 in. 1½-in.-wide French wired ribbon, leaf color (optional)
- 1¼-in.-diameter (3.2cm) filigree stamping
- small teardrops (magatamas)
  5g for flower
  5g for fringe (optional)
- 10g seed beads, size 11º (optional)
- 28-gauge craft wire
- pin back
- Nymo B
- beading needles, #10
Tools: wire cutters

4. When you reach the stem's top, go through the filigree again and repeat steps 1–3 twice, making the center fringe slightly longer than the others.

— *Esther Trusler*

Brooch approach

Create a lovely gemstone flower pin

1. Cut an 18-in. (46cm) piece of craft wire. Center five teardrop-shaped beads on the wire (**photo a**).

2. Pass one end of the wire through the beads once more. Pull each wire end to form a flower shape (**photo b**).

3. Twist the wires together three or four times (**photo c**).

4. Remove the mesh dome from a pin back; set aside the pin back. Center the flower on top of the dome. Pass the wires through one of the holes (**photo d**).

5. Separate the wires. Bring each end through a hole in the dome between two gemstones (**photo e**).

6. Pass each wire through another hole in the dome (**photo f**). Weave the wire between each gemstone.

7. Twist the wire ends together three or four times and trim the excess wire (**photo g**).

8. Cut a 16-in. (41cm) piece of craft wire. String a leaf 1 in. (2.5cm) from the end and twist the shorter wire around the stem. Trim the short wire (**photo h**, p. 134).

9. Place the leaf between two gemstones and pass the wire through a hole in the dome (**photo i**). Bring the wire up and through the dome once more.

10. Bring the wire up through an adjacent pair of gemstones. String a leaf and tack it down as before. Repeat to attach the three remaining leaves (**photo j**). Wrap the end around the core of wires on the back of the dome and trim the excess.

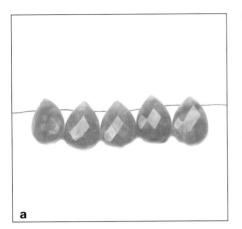

a

b

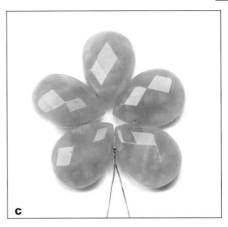

c

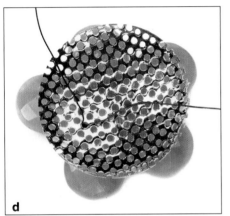

d

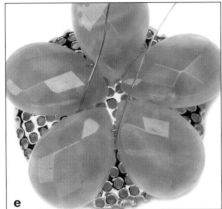

e

f

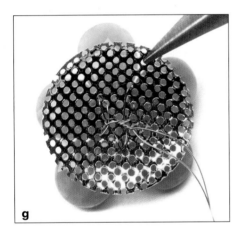

g

11. String two or three rounds, bicones, or rondelles on a head pin. String the head pin through the center of the dome (**photo k**). String beads on another head pin and go through another hole in the dome. Twist the head pins together, bend the wire against the dome, and trim the excess. Repeat with pairs of head pins, until the center is covered.

12. Place the dome in the pin back, positioning it as desired. Gently bend the prongs down around the dome with chainnose pliers (**photo l**).

— *Brenda Schweder*

materials

yellow turquoise brooch

- **5** 18 x 23mm top-drilled teardrop-shaped gemstone beads, yellow turquoise
- **5** 13 x 18mm copper leaf stampings (Eclectica, 262-641-0910, eclecticabeads.com)
- **5-10** 4mm rutilated quartz rondelles
- **10-15** 3mm round onyx beads
- **1¼-in.** (3.2cm) pin back with mesh dome (Designer's Findings, 262-574-1324)
- **5-10** 1½-in. (3.8cm) brass ball-end head pins (Rio Grande, 800-545-6566, riogrande.com)
- **28-gauge** copper craft wire

aquamarine brooch

- **5** 13 x 18mm top-drilled briolettes, synthetic aquamarine
- **5** 13 x 18mm copper leaf stampings
- **5-10** 4mm glass rondelles
- **10-15** 3mm beads (gemstone rounds and bicone crystals)
- **1¼-in.** pin back with mesh dome
- **5-10** 1½-in. brass plain or ball-end head pins
- **28-gauge** copper craft wire

Tools: chainnose pliers, wire cutters

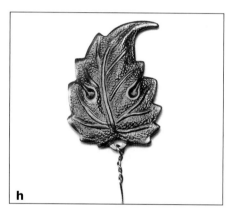

h

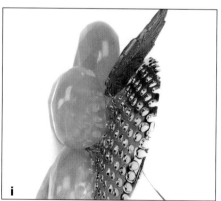

i

j

k

l

Sweater guards

1. Determine the finished length of your sweater guard, using your bracelet size as a guide. (This one is 7½ in./19cm.) Add 5 in. (13cm) and cut a piece of beading wire to that length. String beads and spacers as desired (**photo a**), until the strand is within 2 in. (5cm) of the finished length.

2. String a crimp bead, a seed bead, and half the clasp. Go back through the beads just strung plus one or two more and tighten the wire (**photo b**). Repeat on the other end. Crimp the crimp beads (Basics, p. 8) and trim the excess wire.

3. Trim the head from a head pin and make a plain loop (Basics) at one end or use an eye pin. String ½ in. (1.3cm) of

beads. Make a plain loop above the top bead. If necessary, make the loop perpendicular to the bottom loop; the charm should hang parallel to the clasp (**photo c**).

4. Open the top loop of the dangle and attach it to the eye part of the clasp. Close the loop. Open the bottom loop and attach the charm. Close the loop (**photo d**).

To wear, loop the hook around a button and thread the eye and dangle through the corresponding buttonhole, or wear as a bracelet.

— *Cindy Lutz Kornet*

a

b

c

d

materials

sweater guard 7½ in. (19cm)

- 30-50 assorted 3-8mm beads and spacers
- charm, approx. 10mm (to fit through the sweater's buttonhole)
- 2 seed beads, size 11º
- 2 crimp beads
- hook-and-eye clasp (the hook must fit around the sweater's button and the eye must go through the buttonhole)
- flexible beading wire, .014 or .015
- 1½-in. (3.8cm) head pin or eye pin

Tools: chainnose and roundnose pliers, wire cutters, crimping pliers

Seed beads and sliding briolettes combine to make a fabulous beaded belt

From the hip

Pretty with either your jean skirt or the ubiquitous little black dress, this beaded belt can do double duty as a lariat with lots of wraps. The idea for the belt comes from jewelry designer Katie Hacker, who made the original with brown, gold, and black beads. This simplified version substitutes briolettes for dangles and uses flattened crimps instead of folded ones. A beaded belt is more ornamental than functional — tie it loosely and gently, and you'll enjoy wearing it for years.

1. Wrap a piece of string around your waist or hips. Measure the string, add 30 in. (76cm), and cut two pieces of beading wire to that length (this belt is 53 in./1.3m plus dangles). Set one wire aside.
2. String two 8º beads, a 2mm crimp bead, a spacer, an 8º, a 2mm crimp bead, an 8º, and a soldered jump ring on one wire. Go back through the beads (**photo a**). Crimp both crimp beads

(Basics, p. 8) and trim the excess wire.
3. String a few more 8ºs and 11ºs, until the beaded section is approximately 1¼ in. (3cm). String a 1mm crimp bead (**photo b**). Crimp the crimp bead.
4. String a briolette and a 1mm crimp bead. Crimp the crimp bead approximately ¾ in. (2cm) from the last crimp (**photo c**).
5. String approximately 1¼ in. of assorted 8ºs and 11ºs. String a 1mm crimp bead. Leave about ⅛ in. (3mm) between the last bead and the crimp to allow room for the beads to move. Crimp the crimp bead (**photo d**).
6. Repeat steps 3 and 4 until you are approximately 1¼ in. short of the desired belt length. End with step 3.
7. String ¾ in. of 8ºs and 11ºs. To finish, string two 8ºs, a crimp bead, spacer, 8º, crimp bead, 8º, and a soldered jump ring. Go back through the beads strung, as shown in **photo e** (p. 138). Tighten the wire, crimp the crimp bead, and trim the excess wire.

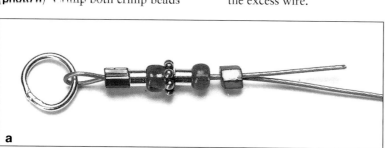

a

b

EDITOR'S NOTE: This belt calls for two sizes of crimp beads — 2mm crimps for the ends and 1mm crimps to space the beads along the belt. The smaller crimps look more delicate, but you can use 2mm crimp beads for the entire project.

c

d

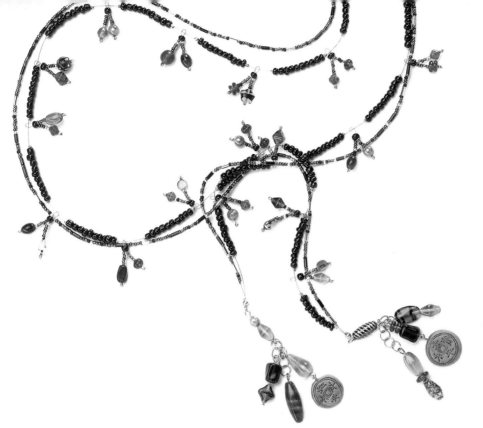

materials
belt 53 in. (1.35m)
• **30-35** jasper briolettes, top-drilled
• 25g seed beads, size 11º,
  five colors (pink, grape, burgundy,
  cocoa, rust)
• 20g seed beads, size 8º, three
  colors (pink, fuchsia, rust)
• Japanese bugle beads, size 1, silver
• **10–20** assorted spacers
• flexible beading wire, .018 or .019
• **8** 2mm tube-shaped crimp beads
• **60–80** 1mm crimp beads, with
  .044 in. hole (Rio Grande,
  800-545-6566)
• **2** 7mm soldered jump rings
• **6** 2½-in. (6cm) head pins
Tools: roundnose and chainnose
  pliers, wire cutters, crimping
  pliers (optional)

e

f

g

h

i

j

8. On the reserved beading wire, string two 8ºs, a crimp bead, an 8º, a crimp bead, an 8º, and one of the jump rings. Go back through the beads (**photo f**). Tighten the wire, crimp the crimp beads, and trim the excess wire.

9. String assorted 11ºs interspersed randomly with bugle beads until this strand is approximately 1 in. (2.5cm) shorter than the first strand (**photo g**).

10. String an 8º, a crimp bead, an 8º, a crimp bead, an 8º, and the soldered jump ring at the end of the belt. Go back through the last beads strung (**photo h**). The top strand should be about ½ in. (1.3cm) shorter than the bottom strand. Add or remove beads, if necessary. Crimp the crimp beads and trim the excess wire.

11. To make dangles for the ends, string six head pins with assorted beads and spacers (**photo i**).

12. Make the first half of a wrapped loop (Basics) above the end beads and connect three dangles to one of the jump rings (**photo j**). Complete the wraps. Attach the remaining dangles to the jump ring at the other end.

— *Katie Hacker and Naomi Fujimoto*

Dainty dragonfly pendants are easy to make and get a great response

materials

dragonfly pendant
- 4 10mm pressed glass dagger beads
- 4 4mm Swarovski bicone crystals
- 7 triangle beads, size 10º
- 6 in. (15cm) 24-gauge sterling silver wire, half hard
- head pin

for necklace add:
- 6 4mm Swarovski bicone crystals
- 12 in. (30cm) 24-gauge sterling silver wire
- 16-in (41cm) chain
- 2 6mm split rings
- lobster-claw clasp

for earrings add:
- second set of pendant beads
- 2 earring findings

Tools: roundnose and chainnose pliers, wire cutters; split ring pliers (optional)

Dragonfly charm

1. String the dragonfly tail on the head pin, alternating a crystal and a triangle bead three times. Cut the wire off, leaving ⅜ in. (1cm) and make a plain loop (Basics, p. 8).

2. For the body, make a right-angle bend in the wire 2 in. (5cm) from one end. On the long end, string a triangle, two dagger beads, a triangle, the loop of the head pin, a triangle, two daggers, and a triangle (**photo a**).

3. Gently curve the section of strung beads into a circle around a jaw of your roundnose pliers so the long end of wire crosses the 2-in. section at the bend (**photo b**).

4. Hold the circle of beads firmly and wrap the end around the 2-in. piece two to three times, keeping the wraps close. The first wrap should be right on the bend (**photo c**). Trim the tail close and press it against the vertical wire with chainnose pliers.

5. String one crystal on the 2-in. wire. Then make a small wrapped loop above the crystal (Basics).

Earrings

For earrings, make a second dragonfly. Then open the loops on the earring findings (Basics) and hang a dragonfly on each earring. Close the loops.

Necklace

1. Cut two 2-in. lengths of wire and start a wrapped loop on one end of each.

2. Hook both loops on the loop above the dragonfly and complete the wraps.

3. String a crystal on each wire and start a wrapped loop against each crystal. Hook a half-inch (1.3cm) length of chain on each loop before completing the wraps (**photo d**).

4. Repeat step 1, hooking a wrapped loop to each end of the chain. Then repeat step 3.

5. Repeat step 4, this time hooking a 6-in. (15cm) length of chain above each crystal.

6. String a split ring on one end of the necklace and attach the clasp to the other end with another split ring.

— *Irina Miech*

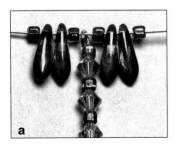

The ring's the thing

String a multitude of crystal and silver rings

silver ring

1. Determine the finished length of your ring, add 3 in. (7.6cm), and cut a piece of beading wire to that length. Center 3mm and 4mm beads on the wire, and string seed beads on each side until the ring is the desired length (**photo a**).

2. String a crimp bead on one wire, and pass the other wire through the crimp bead in the opposite direction. Go through an additional seed bead on each side (**photo b**). Pull the wires tight and check the fit. Add or remove seed beads, if necessary.

3. Make a folded crimp (Basics, p. 8) and trim the excess wire (**photo c**).

daisy ring

1. Determine the finished length of your ring and add 3 in. Double that measurement, and cut a piece of elastic to that length. Center a twisted-wire beading needle on the elastic and tape the ends together.

2. String an accent bead, a crystal, and an accent bead. String spacers until the ring is the desired length (**photo d**). Check the fit, and add or remove spacers, if necessary.

3. Pull the ends together and tie a surgeon's knot (Basics and **photo e**). Glue the knot and trim the ends. Gently pull the ring to slide the knot into the accent bead's hole.

double-strand cube ring

1. Determine the finished length of your ring and add 3 in. Cut two pieces of elastic to that length. Thread a twisted-wire beading needle on one strand of elastic.

2. String a squaredelle and about 1½ in. (3.8cm) of seed beads on the elastic. String two squaredelles, a cube, and a squaredelle (**photo f**, p. 142). Remove the needle.

3. Thread the needle on the second piece of elastic and pass it through the first squaredelle. String a length of seed beads equal to the first strand. Pass the needle through the squaredelles, cube, and squaredelle (**photo g**).

4. Check the fit, and add or remove seed beads from each strand, if necessary. Pull the ends together and tie a surgeon's knot (**photo h**). Glue the knot and trim the ends. Hide the knot between the two squaredelles.

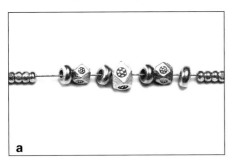

a

b

c

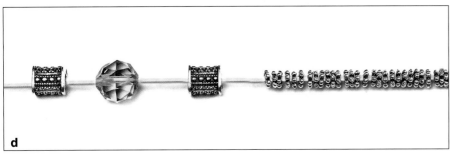

d

e

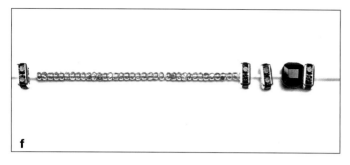

f

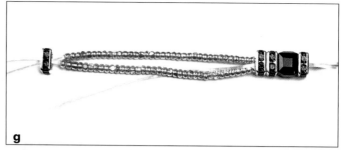

g

materials

silver ring
- 4mm cube, Hill Tribes silver
- **2** 3mm cubes, Hill Tribes silver
- **4** 3mm discs, silver
- 1g faceted seed beads, size 11º, silver
- crimp bead
- flexible beading wire, .014 or .015

daisy ring
- 6-8mm round crystal
- **2** 5 x 6mm large-hole accent beads
- **60-70** 2mm flat spacers
- ribbon elastic
- twisted-wire beading needle, medium
- G-S Hypo Cement

double-strand cube ring
- 6mm cube-shaped crystal
- **4** 6mm squaredelles
- 1g faceted seed beads, size 11º, silver
- ribbon elastic
- twisted-wire beading needle, medium
- G-S Hypo Cement

dazzling double-strand ring
- 8mm cube-shaped crystal
- **2** 8mm squaredelles
- **2** 4mm bicone crystals
- 1g faceted seed beads, size 11º, silver
- crimp bead
- flexible beading wire, .014 or .015

Tools: crimping pliers, wire cutters, scissors

h

i

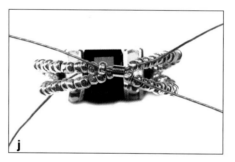

j

k

dazzling double-strand ring

1. Determine the finished length of your ring, add 3 in., and cut two pieces of beading wire to that length. Center a bicone, a squaredelle, a cube, a squaredelle, and a bicone over both wires. Separate the wires, and string seed beads on each end of each wire until the ring is the desired length (**photo i**).

2. String a crimp bead over both wires on one end, and pass the other ends through the crimp bead in the opposite direction. Go through an additional seed bead on each strand (**photo j**). Pull the wires tight and check the fit. Add or remove seed beads, if necessary.

3. Make a folded crimp and trim the excess wire (**photo k**).

— *Carolyn Sheahan*

STANDARD RING SIZES

SIZE 5	2 in.	5.1cm
SIZE 6	2⅛ in.	5.4cm
SIZE 7	2¼ in.	5.7cm
SIZE 8	2⅜ in.	6.0 cm

Making headlines

Attach beads to a comb or bobby pin for a delicate hair accessory

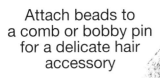

a

b

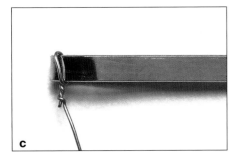

c

d

materials

comb
- **18–20** assorted charms, crystals, and gemstones
- metal hair comb
- 24-gauge wire

bobby pin
- **8–10** assorted charms, crystals, and gemstones
- **6–12** seed beads, size 11º
- bobby pin
- 28-gauge wire

Tools: chainnose pliers, wire cutters

Comb

1. Cut a 12 in. (30cm) piece of 24-gauge wire. Starting between the first two prongs, wrap the wire tightly around the comb's base two or three times (**photo a**).

2. String one or two beads and wrap the wire tightly around the base (**photo b**). To position beads vertically, pull the wire down behind the bead (see inset) and make a wrap just below the bead.

Continue wiring beads until you reach the end of the comb. Wrap the wire around the comb two more times and trim the excess. Using chainnose pliers, tuck the wire end under the wraps.

Bobby pin

1. Cut a 12 in. piece of 28-gauge wire. Wrap it around the bobby pin near the fold, leaving a 1-in. (2.5cm) tail. Twist the tail and working wire together tightly several times. Trim the excess wire from the tail (**photo c**).

2. String beads as desired, wrapping the wire around the bobby pin between each bead or pair of beads (**photo d**). To finish, trim the excess wire and tuck the end under the wraps.

— *Naomi Fujimoto*

Contributors

Pam Arion works for TierraCast. For more information on additional designs, visit tierracast.com or e-mail her at info@tierracast.com.

Linda Augsburg is the Editor-at-Large for *Bead&Button* magazine. Contact her at editor@kalmbach.com

Rupa Balachandar offers a large selection of silver pendants and beads on her website, rupab.com. E-mail her at rupa_balachandar@hotmail.com

Paulette Biedenbender is a former Editorial Associate of *BeadStyle* magazine. She owns a store, Bead Needs, in Franklin, Wisconsin. Contact her in care of editor@beadstyle.com.

Karin Buckingham is a former Associate Editor of *BeadStyle* magazine. Contact her in care of editor@beadstyle.com.

Nina Cooper is the founding designer and president of Nina Designs Ltd. She writes regularly for the trade on a range of subjects. You can see more of her work at ninadesigns.com or contact her at 800-336-NINA.

Gloria Farver can be contacted via e-mail at DesignsByGWiz@wi.rr.com.

Lois Fetters can be contacted via e-mail at geanfet@riverview.net or by mail at 1227 Birch Drive, White Cloud, Michigan 49349.

Naomi Fujimoto is an Associate Editor at *BeadStyle* magazine. Contact her at editor@beadstyle.com

Katie Hacker is a jewelry designer. Contact her at katie@katiehacker.com or view her website, katiehacker.com.

Cathy Hansen-Vandenberg has many kits available. Contact her via e-mail at cathyvandenb@aol.com or by phone at 248-348-4926.

Dawn Hardy can be contacted via e-mail at dawn@zunibearblankets.com or by phone at 208-263-3605.

Maryann Humes has a website, buyMair.com. Contact her by via e-mail at info@buyMair.com or by phone at 239-784-2682.

Diane Hyde sells kits necklaces through her company, Designer's Findings. E-mail her at dianehdesigns@execpc.com or call her, 262-574-1324. Send a fax to 262-547-8799.

Juana Jelen can be contacted at sales@pacificsilverworks.com.

Diane Jolie is the former Managing Editor of *Bead&Button* magazine. Contact her at editor@beadandbutton.com.

Anne Kloss is a renowned beader and instructor extraordinaire from Waukesha, Wisconsin. E-mail her at annekloss@mac.com.

Jane Konkel is an Associate Editor for *BeadStyle* magazine. Contact her at editor@beadstyle.com.

Alice Korach is the founding Editor of *Bead&Button* magazine. Her website is lostwaxglass.com.

Cindy Lutz Kornet has self-pubished a book *Art and Soul a spiritual approach to crafts*. Contact her via e-mail at artsoul@comcast.net. Her website is artandsoulbycin.com.

Melody MacDuffee is a jewelry designer. E-mail her at writersink@msn.com or contact Melody at 6200 Airport Blvd. #99, Mobile, Alabama 36608.

Louise Malcolm is a former Contributing Editor to *Bead&Button* magazine.

Irina Miech owns Eclectica in Brookfield, Wisconsin. Her website is eclecticabeads.com; you can e-mail her at eclecticainfo@sbcglobal.net.

Anne Mitchell specializes in chain patterns and metal working techniques. View her website at annemitchell.net or e-mail her at anne@annemitchell.net.

Anna Nehs is an Associate Editor at *Bead&Button* magazine. Contact her at editor@beadandbutton.com.

Stacey Neilson brings her jewelry designs from Ireland. Contact her via e-mail at stacey@yellowbrickroad.ie. Her business' website is yellowbrickroad.ie.

Debbie Nishihara is an Associate Editor at *Bead&Button* magazine. Contact her at editor@kalmbach.com.

Kim Otterbein can be contacted via e-mail at kimodesign@msn.com or 11 Constitution St., Bristol, Rhode Island 02809. Her phone number is 401-253-1188.

Cheryl Phelan is an Associate Editor at *Bead&Button* magazine. Contact her at editor@beadandbutton.com.

Candice St. Jacques is the Editor-in-Chief of Kalmbach Books. Contact her at books@kalmbach.com.

Brenda Schweder offers fashion-savvy jewelry kits on her website, BrendaSchweder.com. Contact her via e-mail at b@BrendaSchweder.com

Carolyn Sheahan can be reached in care of *BeadStyle*.

Esther Trusler has kits available for her brooches at EZ Knit. Contact EZ Knit at 1-800-246-2644 or 165 N. Main, Colville, WA 99114. E-mail address is ezknit.com.

Judy Walker has been beading for over 35 years. She can be contacted at judywalker@pobox.com,

Beth Wheeler can be contacted in care of *BeadStyle*.

Julie Young works for TierraCast. For more information on additional designs, visit tierracast.com or e-mail her at info@tierracast.com.